Snapshots of a War Bride's Life

Joy A. Beebe

Snapshots of a War Bride's Life

———◄O►———

A 1940s historical and sentimental account of a young English girl and her family, living and working during WWII. While enduring frightening bombing raids, sleeping under a table and watching London burn from afar, Joy meets and marries American soldier Carl. After the War, they leave Britain with a two-year old son. Joy is just 22; she does not yet know that she will have very little connection with her homeland for decades. After their troop ship postwar journey from Southampton, England to New York and train trip across the US, the couple arrive in Salem, Oregon with $10 to begin their life in America.

———◄O►———

Snapshots of a War Bride's Life

© 2024 by Joy A. Beebe

All rights reserved.

6th Edition, 76th Anniversary of Arrival in America – February 14, 2024.

5th Edition, 78th Wedding Anniversary – April 28, 2023

4th Edition, 70th Anniversary of WWII – July 2015

3rd Edition – May 2013

2nd Edition – June 2012

1st Edition, 67th Wedding Anniversary – April 28, 2012

Print ISBN: 979-8-9900829-0-8

EBook ISBN: 979-8-9900829-1-5

Contents

Dedication

A dedication to my family
On both sides of the Atlantic Ocean
With Love

I would like to thank my children, Philip, Jennifer, Barbara and Vivian for their support and enthusiasm when I was writing my stories. Special thanks go to Jennifer and her granddaughter, DaraLyn, who helped with the final stages of the 1st Edition, Barbara who advised in the 2nd Edition, all daughters, who advised in the 3rd Edition, and my youngest daughter, Vivian, who led the effort for the 4th Edition of this book.

My children have encouraged me to write about growing up in England and my travels. I started to write earlier, and now that I am 86 years old I am ready to share my story. I wish to say that these stories were written at different times and not in chronological order. I apologize for repetitions.

I am also grateful for the interest and friendship of my writing class and my French teacher, GwenEllyn Anderson, who convinced me that my stories should be shared.

Joy A. Beebe

Now they resolved to go back to their own land, because the years have a kind of emptiness when we spend too many of them on a foreign shore.

But, if we do return, we find that the native air has lost its invigorating quality, and that life has shifted its reality to the spot where we have deemed ourselves only temporary residents.

Thus, between two countries, we have none at all.

Nathaniel Hawthorne
1804-1864
From *The Marble Faun*

Foreword

By daughter
Barbara Anne

On April 28th 2023, with the publishing of this 5th Edition, Joy Alicia Beaver Beebe was laid to rest with our father, Carl Stewart Beebe at Oregon's National Veteran's Cemetery, Willamette National on what would have been their 78th Wedding Anniversary.

Her Lasting Legacy

*N*o one could have known at the time how my mother Joy's first edition of this book, published over a decade ago, would be so symbolic of the final chapter of her life. She captured her English and American memories—living on two continents and bridging families on both.

She described her childhood trauma of listening to the radio, announcing that Hitler had taken Poland and was now after the Brits. She spoke firsthand of adversities and deprivation of living through the bombing and Blitz of London during World War II. She explained the years of sleeping with her family under a netted table to be protected from bomb shrapnel. She depicted her sad teenage years; as her father dies, she is forced to decline a chemist scholarship and, at age 16, begin her adult work life to support a family of four.

She highlighted her young adult years with a brighter vision of falling in love, marrying an American GI, celebrating the victory of a six-year world war and the birth of her first child.

Yet at the end of the war, with difficult times in England, it became necessary for Joy and Carl to move to America. Without the blessing of her mother, they sailed west across the ocean toward a life unknown. It was difficult. But with the love and support of her husband, she adapted rapidly to her new life in Oregon. She became successful in business, valued in her community, and, most important, cherished by her family. She prided herself living decades in her beloved home on Sunset Avenue, a place that her talented husband renovated many times to make it just as she wanted.

Following the first release of this memoir, her final chapter was about to unfold; the chapter that would allow her to retrace all previous ones and share her life with a broader audience, from her WWII Generation to today's youth.

After receiving Mom's book on April 28, 2012, I was deeply moved and affected by her drive, determination, and life story. Inspired by her words, Mom and I would share the next decade together on a special journey. It was a chapter in her life, at the best time in mine, to get to know her and an opportunity to share in her joys, understand her hardships, and document her legacy.

Mom was excited with the interest and a natural process opened for her to share her story.

Statesman Journal Memorial News ~ 2012

Early May, an Oregon Capitol City Statesman journalist arrived at her Sunset Avenue home for a Memorial Day front page article. After *listening an hour, the journalist inquired, "Where is this 'black market' wedding dress you speak about?" Mom smiled, walked down the hallway and out it came from the back of the closet—for the first time in decades. "It was only intended to protect my china during our sail to America," she explained. "However, after two weeks of rough Atlantic seas on a troop ship and a 3,000-mile train journey to the West Coast, the china was disappointingly reduced to shards." No longer needed, the dress had found its home, hidden in the closet. Now, the impromptu 'unveiling' of the dress in this interview became her signature and on a journey that would create her lasting legacy.*

When my brother, Philip, received her book, he reached out to Mom about the National WWII War Brides Association, wondering if she was interested. Having coordinated activities for 60 years with the local war brides Salem Accent Club, she was eager to explore this organization. She asked me to reach out and, immediately, she was invited to join.

Mosaic of the "Kiss Statue" Times Square,
New York City ~ 2012

During one of our first interactions with the war brides, they mentioned The Spirit of '45, a national organization formed to recognize the WWII Generation for their courage, sacrifice, spirit, unity, and service. After connecting with their leadership, Mom was chosen to be the honorary WWII delegate at their annual August celebration. It started with the Kiss Statue in New York, then on to the National WWII Memorial in Washington, DC, and concluded with her first national War Bride reunion in Boston. With the fanfare of media, jumbotrons, journalists, citizen interest, and thousands of helium balloons– her story began to take on new meaning.

Her concept of a personal memoir to share with her immediate family quickly advanced to one of sharing her experience of the time with those interested in WWII. Featured that August in the Wall Street Journal and Washington Post, her East Coast experience clearly surpassed the thrill of her own arrival at the Statute of Liberty back in 1948. At an on-stage moment with Good-Morning America Anchor, Josh Elliott, her dress was showcased in Times Square. Continuing her delegation role, she traveled on to the Washington DC WWII Memorial for the official Spirit of '45 Day and then to Boston, where her 'black market' wedding dress was exhibited for the first time. She was stunned and simply glowed as this series of events launching her memoir beyond her dreams. Little did she think that these new experiences would be a time-capsule of reliving the best memories of her early life.

New York City, Times Square ~ 2012

In 2013, her story expanded. When I returned from a February national Spirit of '45 leadership conference in San Diego, I shared with Mom the idea of lobbying Oregon leaders to recognize the WWII Generation with a proclamation. Working with our state senator and the city of Portland mayor, we began a process to honor Spirit of '45 Day. It was timely as Oregon, the 33rd state in the nation, was now constructing a 33' obelisk WWII Memorial on its state capitol grounds. I proposed we declare the second Sunday of every August in honor the WWII Generation.

In consideration of my request, the Portland Mayor invited Mom and me to testify at the City Council. Mom spoke about living through the 1940's Blitz and her father losing his life from gas-effects of both WWI and WWII. She shared that at age 16, as the oldest child, she needed to work full-time to support the family. She explained how her employer, the British government, sent her on special assignment to the English Channel on June 5, 1944 to dig potatoes. She never remembered digging any potatoes, only witnessing thousands of troops singing and marching to the beaches on June 6 (later branded, D-Day). She ended her testimony with a few words about crossing the rough Atlantic sea and arriving at the Statute of Liberty aboard a cracked troop ship on Valentine's Day 1948 with only $10.

The Oregon Veteran's Committee was mesmerized. Our state senator exclaimed, 'Why a proclamation? Why not make it the law!' That May, a unanimous vote from The Senate and House of Representatives passed the bill, making Oregon the first state in the nation to enact Spirit of '45 Day and make part of state statute.

In June of 2013, Mom arrived at Governor Kitzhaber's "Oval Office" for the bill-signing and was greeted by the Governor, military Generals, legislators, and other state officials.

Shortly after the signing, with Mom as our honorary board member, I started the Oregon Spirit of '45 nonprofit to observe the second Sunday in August as a day of remembrance and inspiration.

Oregon Governor's Office ~ 2013

In February of 2015, at the dedi-cation of the 25' Kiss Statute in San Diego in front of the USS Midway, Mom wowed the press in a pow-erful and grateful one-minute mes-sage about how the Americans saved the Brits in WWII. For the nation's Memorial Day parade, she rallied and actively nurtured the Spirit of '45 youth team as they raised money to travel and parade in Washington, DC.

USS Midway, San Diego ~ 2015

The Spirit of '45 mission became core to her endless conversations, inter-views, and engagements – a natural conduit to share her English war bride story. She enjoyed Veteran's Day, riding annually in and waving from an Army camouflage jeep, surrounded by cadets marching the parade route. She often joined U.S. Senator Ron Wyden, a visible parade supporter who honored his father, an expert in psychological warfare intelligence during WWII.

Albany Veteran's Day Parade ~ 2017

Mom was encouraged to share her story in book signings, at author fairs, and during interviews with journal-ists, and historians. As the 70th An-niversary of the end of WWII ap-proached, she was contacted by one of the soldiers of my father's 6811th Army Detachment. He was looking for contributions for a special exhibit at Hall Place and Gardens in Kent. Hall Place is a Tudor home built in the six-teenth century for the London Mayor. From 1943-1945, Hall Place became a US-occupied remote site where my father was stationed during WWII. Mom could never have imagined that this unique encounter would lead to a lasting home for her "hidden in the closet" wedding dress and become her legacy.

Hall Place, 2015 ~ Present

In August of 2015, Mom stood in awe at the extensively restored Hall Place with magnificent galleries, a beautiful sub-tropical glasshouse, and award-winning royal gardens on the banks of the river Cray. Inside the Hall, Mom was enchanted, viewing the exhibit of her on-loan wedding dress covered in a glass case. Her memories at that point returned to an old, dilapidated estate home—a guarded site with iron gates that no one during WWII was allowed to enter. She knew the Americans were serving but my father, sworn to secrecy, did not speak about his role or anything he knew about their mission. It was at this anniversary the top secret Santa Fe Ultra Operation was revealed. They disclosed the Bletchley Park connected

Y-Station (Hall Place) of 190 GIs intercepting encoded messages sent by the Germans. Only now would we know how my father, who died in October 1995, helped to curtail the end of WWII by two years.

The next few years Mom would travel to meet her dress, often on exhibit at war bride reunions, displayed with a few other foreign wedding dresses of her war bride sisters. It was showcased on the Queen Mary in Long Beach, in the WWII Museum in New Orleans, as well as San Diego and Las Vegas. She experienced conversations with WWII enthusiasts, TV and newspaper reporters, and graduate students. Periodically, she appeared in TV clips, newspaper articles and graduate theses presentations. In 2022, she had a special opportunity to share her fashion expertise with a professor at UC, Davis, who released a book on the scarcity of clothing in WWII; Mom was referenced or quoted over 30 times.

New Orleans WWII Museum ~ 2013

Oregon Governor and Adjutant ~ 2019

In May of 2019, Mom was invited to join Oregon Governor Brown and Adjutant General Stencil on Armed Services Day in Salem to share her story with the public on the State capitol grounds. With Military honors, the Army Band and flyovers, mom had quite the sendoff for her next day—jet-setting to London to be interviewed by 'Queen-knighted' Sir Tony Robinson. In 2020, her 8-minute story aired in a BBC History of Britain miniseries, covering periods of Tudor, Georgian, Victorian and WWII. In her finest debut, the filming took place in Bexleyheath, Kent, both at her childhood home and Hall Place and Gardens.

Sir Tony Robinson, Hall Place ~ 2019

I believe Mom knew this was likely her last time to stand on her homeland soil. Once again and for the last time, she would view her wedding dress in its glass case, with her book displayed at the hem. The dress, featured on the top floor of the Great Hall, stood stately as a part of their permanent 75th Anniversary exhibit. It represents the love and lives of 190 GIs who, over an 18-month period, broke enemy-code to end the war. As she stood still in time at the intersection of past and present, she realized her legacy was set—her generation remembered.

By 2022 with the world recovering from the COVID pandemic, Mom continued to remain active and attentive. After her birthday wishes in August, she diligently continued her seventh year as the national War Bride's "Sunshine Lady," mailing birthday cards (all handwritten) to sister war brides and their "war babies." But we also knew that time was becoming precious.

In mid-October, just returning from her English homeland, I was able to support her in meeting with another WWII-focused journalist who wanted to hear her story. This military journalist was the granddaughter of another WWII war bride. Mom and I settled in her Sunset bay-window sitting area in front of the kitchen where we had gathered so many times over the years.

Lasting Legacy Article ~ 2022

She loved this special place, on her favorite love seat. As we jumped online to meet Crystal, I was pleased to see Mom so well-prepared. I should have known she would be as she took coursework all her life, with a focus on Writing and French over the past decade. As Crystal asked each question, Mom seemed a beat ahead, appropriately anticipating the dialogue. For nearly an hour, Mom shared her war bride-Spirit of '45 story in her wonderful remanent of a British accent, softened by years of living in the U.S. The conversation was rich, caring, and genuine–character traits we all came to love and appreciate in Mom.

As with all of us, we carry joys and burdens of our time on this earth. Mom too, had so many moments of happiness mixed with the trials of life. As she entered her remaining time with us, we were blessed with hospice care and the grace of one of their nurses named Scott. Scott had first visited Mom in early October, immediately building rapport and trust with her. He had a way of being compassionate and charming while at the same time, direct and honest. On his second visit, later in October, I met him for the first time. Scott was able to ask Mom a deeply caring question, "What is it that troubles you?" It was a transcendental moment. As she hypnotically stared at him for what seemed an awkward amount of time, she solemnly stated, "I left her–I deserted my mother." Sitting in Mom's bay-window, I sensed a heavy weight in her voice and in the same moment, a sigh of relief. And then, Scott gracefully led her to a place that allowed her to "let go." In a single moment, Scott, as if sent by angels, had given Mom the peace that for so long she had sought.

She seemed to release the regret of leaving her mother, freeing her from the 'no blessing' burden she had carried 75 years, since sailing to America.

I felt so very grateful for the hospice experience that allowed her to release this sorrow of her past–perhaps purposeful in writing her book and why her final chapter is so important to her family and to me.

On Tuesday evening, after the interview with Crystal and visit from Scott, we once again continued with our tradition of "wine time on Sunset," as Mom, her next-door neighbor, Lani, and I sat around the sitting area, sharing wine and nibbles–so enjoying each other's company.

The next day, almost as if the sheer release of this secret was let go, she had a stroke. I found her in the bathroom, stary-eyed and silent. I asked, "Can you hear me?" She said "Yes." I asked, "Are you in pain," she said "No." These were her last words.

The paramedics arrived soon after and helped her into bed. As they left, Lani and I stood over her. We stared at each other, then at her. In an instant, we realized it was time to call Scott. He quickly arrived and stayed half the day to ensure her comfort and provide support to the two of us. Soon my sisters, Jennifer and Vivian, arrived as our mother lay quietly resting in bed. We sent word to the family to gather on Sunset Avenue to be with Mom in her final moments.

In the wee hours of Sunday morning, October 30, with her loving descendants arriving over the weekend, Mom restfully drifted away in her home of 65 years. Sitting with her were three of her loving granddaughters.

Her final snapshot was as Mom would have loved it to be. On her left was her great-granddaughter, Mariah, holding Mom's right hand while cradling Mom's great-great granddaughter, Vada. At her right was her granddaughter, Stephanie, holding Mom's right hand and reading this book to her ... 'Snapshots of a War Bride's Life.'

As Mom traveled and met with people to share her story, she was supported by a exceptionally dedicated and devoted team...well, a sisterhood.

Joy with daughter, Jennifer Joy ~ 2015

On the home front, her ready and alert daughters were naturally in place to support her as she continued her unforeseen journey. My older sister, Jennifer Joy, was her rock. She ensured Mom's basic needs were met, doctor appointments were managed, and the bills were paid timely. My younger sister, Vivian Elaine was her medical advocate and consummate worldwide travel companion. Mom was proud to have her youngest beside her, guiding her medical needs—the pharmacist-educated child who was able to follow through with Mom's 1941 lost opportunity to become a chemist. Her thoughtful neighbor, Lani, epitomized southern hospitality with her unwavering support and care of Mom for over 30 years. No one outside the family could have cared for her more, been more available to her or achieved the trusting status for Mom's social and emotional needs than this lovely neighbor, AKA daughter, with such a big heart.

Times Square with Barbara, Lani and Vivian ~ 2012

Two other special women in Mom's life were her "adopted" daughter, Sue, and admired first grade schoolteacher, Mrs. O (Pat). Each cherished our mother and treated her like royalty. From her teenage years, Sue glowed with pride and fondly referred to our parents as, Ma and Pa Beeb. For over a decade, Pat consistently boosted Mom's school volunteer spirit and viewed our mother as hers, telling her students and colleagues daily, "Everyone should have a 'My Mrs. Beebe' in their lives."

It was my role to plan the celebrations and moments of recognition. In 2015, we had a wonderful 90th birthday celebration, attended by over 100 family and friends. In 2021, after the pandemic had finally waned, we celebrated her 96th with everyone meeting at Sunset to share their stories. In 2022, for her 97th birthday, she received over 150 cards from around the world, which was so fitting since Mom never missed a chance to send someone—anyone —a card, even for the simplest of things. A blizzard of love surrounded her with flowers, cards, emails, photos, videos, and phone calls.

During her 97th birthday celebration, the National War Bride reunion was being held in Niagara Falls. Unable to cross from West to East Coast America to attend, she experienced a truly heartfelt moment when all her war bride sisters called her by surprise at her home to sing "happy birthday." She glowed for days, perhaps even through her last days with us.

National War Brides, Boston ~ 2012

Over the months since her passing, we have gathered for farewells and sorted through Mom's many possessions. We discovered family treasures which have found their way into the homes of all her relatives. Her English families, featuring beloved younger brother Geoffrey and prized sister-in law, Carol—were hosted in a special video call for an extended farewell. They enjoyed walking through and experiencing her home one last time from across the pond, remembering their time with Mom throughout the decades.

One of the treasured possessions uncovered included commemorative pins from Queen

Elizabeth's Coronation that none of us knew about. They were sent in the Spring of 1953 by her mother, Reneé Therin Beaver, and meant to be worn by each of Mom's children on Queen Elizabeth's Coronation Day in June.

Queen Coronation Pins ~ 1953

This past February, we had Mom's Celebration of Life at Sunset, where family and friends spent hours sharing their memories of her, including Scott from hospice. He shared how Mom had touched him, with just their few encounters. After the estate sale of her possessions, we discovered that seven cups and saucers of her beloved, long-lived china remained; ironically, one for each of the Sunset-connected sisters. On March 14, the Sunset "sisters" met at the Salem airport restaurant Mom had owned and managed for years, The Flight Deck. Each sister was presented with a Desert Rose teacup and saucer, and we all toasted our dear mother and friend, Joy.

on, Wednesday Morning, July 18

PFC. and Mrs. Carl S. Beebe (Joy Beaver) who were married in Bexley Heath, England. The groom is the son of Mr. and Mrs. Roy Beebe of Salem, and his wife is the daughter of Mrs. R. Beaver. The couple spent their honeymoon in Surrey. Pictured with the bridal couple is Betty Croucher, bridesmaid.

Salem Man Weds English Girl

Mr. and Mrs. Roy A. Beebe, 2475 Broadway st., announce the marriage of their son, PFC Carl S. Beebe to Miss Joy A. Beaver, daughter of Mrs. R. Beaver, of 47 Marlborough Road, Bexley Heath, England, and the late Mr. W. J. Beaver. The Rev. F. Moore officiated.

The bride, who was given away by her brother, Mr. Anthony Beaver, wore a white satin dress with long veil, and carried a bouquet of roses, carnations and lilies of the valley. Her silver locket and chain were the gift of the bride groom.

The bridesmaids, two dressed in pink crepe, the other in blue crepe, were Miss Margaret Mercer, Miss Barbara Hill and Miss Betty Croucher. Sergeant Herbert Jaquist was best man.

After a reception at the home of the bride's mother, the couple left for a short honeymoon in Surrey, the bride traveling in a navy blue costume.

Wedding Announcement in Salem newspaper ~ July 18, 1945

INTRODUCTION: A NEW LIFE IN AMERICA

I am often asked about my thoughts on marrying an American soldier during a war and immigrating to the United States of America. It's a hard question to answer and I have to admit that I am not too sure that I thought too deeply about it at the time. I knew I wanted to marry Carl and that he felt the same way. We loved each other. Though my mother had lots of doubts, she liked him and so did the rest of my family: brothers, grandma and aunts. He had endeared himself to all of them; a visit from him was always a pleasure.

What is hard to explain to others so many years later is that we rarely thought of the future. Today, there is constant planning, preparation for the years ahead, schools, colleges, travel and other opportunities. Then, it was 1945; England had been at war for almost six years. We had been bombed repeatedly by German aircraft and were at the mercy of V1 (Doodlebugs) and V2 rockets. Our home had been badly damaged and those of friends and neighbors had been destroyed; some neighbors had been killed. We suffered severe shortages of food, clothes and household goods. We had been deprived of proper help with our education and ran a constant risk of being called to serve in the army, women too.

Carl Stewart Beebe ~ 1945

Joy Alicia Beaver Beebe ~ 1945

My father had died in 1941. He had been gassed in the Great War (1914-1918) and in ill health for most of his life. My brother Tony, who was in the Marines, suffered a leg injury during parachute training that caused him difficulty walking. Grandma Therin had been evacuated to the country to be safe from air raids. Auntie Alice's office around St. Paul Cathedral, where she had worked for 50 years, had burned to the ground during a three-day incendiary raid by the Germans. Grandpa Beaver had died from pneumonia after checking his house on the Kentish Coast. It was next door to a small, though busy, airport used by the R.A.F. and he had been told by the government to leave it because of the danger of invasion, etc. Though others had far worse tragedies, we wondered what else the future would hold.

Getting married was a happy and exciting event to plan for. Even though my mother was often quite upset about it, I have her to thank for making it a happy event; she even made dresses for the three bridesmaids. We had a lovely formal wedding in St. John's Church in Welling with family, friends and lots of G.I.s—soldiers from Carl's unit. It was not my first choice. This church had been badly damaged during the air raids, had a leaky roof and all the stained glass windows were shattered and boarded with wood. I had hoped for Christchurch on the Bexleyheath Broadway as it was larger and more beautiful inside. But it turned out that I lived just over the border of the Bexleyheath parish and out of their area.

Tony found me a wedding dress and veil on the black market (I've kept the dress to this day, but had to return the veil). The mother of his friend, Derek Woolgar, made me a proper English wedding cake, a fruit cake and hard icing. This was probably another black market deal since dried fruits, eggs, butter, flour, and sugar. In fact, all the things necessary to make the cake had been either rationed or nonexistent for years. There was a war on, remember? Ma ordered a hired car to take me back and forth to the church and a reception was held in our front room for family and a few friends. Believe it or not, that was only the third or fourth time I had ever ridden in a car!

It snowed that day as we went into the church. As Tony walked me down the aisle, his shoulders were snow-covered. But when we came out of the church, the sun was bright and we had some good pictures taken by Frank Penney, one of Carl's army buddies.

Afterwards, Carl and I took off for the weekend to Arundel, Surrey on the train. Arundel is a lovely English village and the country hotel where we stayed served more fancy food than we had seen in years. Roast duck for dinner the first night! Carl and I had a good time walking and exploring in the area, visiting an old castle, enjoying being together and not thinking of the war or any of its consequences. He could not get more leave until ten days later. By then, the world was changing!

Our wedding date was Saturday, April 28, 1945, the same weekend that German dictator, Adolf Hitler, ended his life in his Berlin bunker. The Allies (Americans, British, Canadians and soldiers of many other nationalities) advanced almost to Berlin; the end of the war was in sight. By the 8th of May, Germany had surrendered; the Americans, British, and Russians had reached Berlin from all sides. The 'Fuhrer' and other leaders were dead.

Starting May 8, we spent a week in a Bed and Breakfast in Worthing on the South coast of England. So great was our excitement that we paid very little attention to the news. Actually, for years there had been very little news and it was mostly propaganda. Happenings in World War II were not broadcast in detail so imagine our surprise when we started on our journey to find that practically the whole country had taken the day off to celebrate Victory in Europe Day, now known as V.E. Day and a national holiday in France. What should have been a three-hour trip took us all day. We finally arrived at our Bed and Breakfast just in time for dinner, after spending hours waiting on railway platforms and hoping for a train going in our direction. It was all part of our adventure together and we had a lovely week near the seaside. Once again, we found that food was more plentiful in the country, especially near the sea.

Immediately after the war ended, things began to change for us. The danger of missiles had been over for some time and repair work had started on houses that were still standing firmly. Windows were replaced, roofs fixed, and plaster and brick damage repaired; all work was ordered and financed by the government. But there was no extra food in the stores and food rationing continued in England until 1952. It was possible for newlyweds and bombed-out families to get coupons for household goods. Carl and I took advantage of this and bought a table and chairs, sheets and pillowcases and towels—things that could not be bought without the coupons.

There was no way we would be able to get a house of our own in England for many, many years. The waiting list was long and those whose homes had been bombed or totally destroyed (or had very large families) were at the top of the list. So Ma let us have the front room downstairs for our living/ dining room and the back bedroom upstairs. The small bedroom was my younger brother Geoffrey's. Ma had the big front bedroom and we shared the kitchen and bathroom.

Carl was still stationed at Hall Place (close to my home) and I was working for the Inland Revenue Service, Tax Department near the Tower of London.

Hall Place, where Americans listened out for the coded German transmissions

By the end of June, Carl was unexpectedly on his way to Germany with the army of occupation to decipher code to win the war in the Pacific. I was very upset to see him go. It was hard to realize that the fighting was over and that they were taking my new husband away. Hopefully he would be quite safe. The unit left in a large convoy of trucks and jeeps and the officer in charge let me and a couple of other brides ride along as they went slowly through the village of Old Bexley. When they reached the motorway that led to the coast and the departure port, we had to leave. It was a sad parting.

Introduction written June 2004 on vacation in Phoenix, AZ.

Chapter One

EARLY CHILDHOOD
ON SIDCUP HILL

T he following is the story of my brother Tony and me, growing up between two world wars yet a life together in the warmth and comfort of family. My first years were very quiet and happy. I enjoyed living with my mother, father and Tony as well as having my aunts, uncles and cousins visit. Until the end of the 1930s our family was not touched by tragedy. Although we had difficulties making ends meet, the children did not realize it. Our father was ill but we never thought he might die. We were secure. In that security, we had more freedom than today's child.

We didn't have to worry about world problems; our parents did the worrying. We played and learned our lessons and made our own enjoyments. We played in the open air, rode bikes, played board games, completed school lessons and went to Cub Scout and Brownie meetings. There were no televisions or computers, no rock stars to influence us and very few cars on the roads. Our world was a quiet and peaceful place.

I was born in England in 1925, during the depression years between two world wars. They were years when the world was trying to improve the lives of the working man, advance new scientific ventures and live at peace with other countries after suffering the horrors and casualties of the Great War. Before and since, these incidents have not been equaled by any other war in modern times. Many thousands of husbands and fathers were lost or wounded and jobs were very scarce for those who returned.

Joy and Tony with parents William J. and Renée Beaver at
Sidcup Hill ~ 1931

My mother, Renée, was the daughter of French parents who came to England shortly before she was born in January 1894. My grandfather, Augustin (Gaston) Therin, was a woodcarver and furniture maker. At the end of the 19th century, there was very little work in France for those in that trade so he immigrated to England in the hopes of better opportunities. He was born in December 1867 in Rogny de Sept Ecluses, Yonne, France. He had grown up in Paris during the 1870-1871 Siege of Paris by the Germans, a time when Parisians were starved and would eat cats and rats to stay alive. He was only four years old at that time.

As a young man, my grandfather had served two years in the military, compulsory in France in those times. In 1892, he met and married 20-yearold Alice Marie Haubert who lived on the outskirts of a small town called Angouleme on the river Charente in Southwest France. He had been living in the center of the same town, renting a room in a boarding house that still stands at 17 rue Bouillaud. The street was named after a great doctor of the town whose statue stands nearby. There was a cafe and a beautiful fountain decorated with cherubs and flowers at the end of the street. I can imagine the young people gathering there to visit at the end of the day.

The fortress town was built high above the surrounding areas and was encircled by the river Charente with ramparts, stone bulwarks for the defense of the town and built to keep out the invaders of previous centuries. The town was famous for its 12th century St. Pierre Cathedral, a magnificent work of art rising high above the ramparts. There was a Gothic Hotel de Ville, which was originally the palace of a royal princess, Marguerite d'Angouleme, and an impressive food market in the center of the town—where local farmers sold their produce, homemade cheeses, breads, poultry and animals.

Alice Marie and Gaston were married in the Hotel de Ville in the gold-decorated marriage salon and the Catholic Church. As is custom in France, there was both a civil and religious service. Her family had always been market gardeners working the land close to home and selling the produce in the open-air market. She followed this tradition, as well as spending much of her young life caring for her sick mother, Catherine Foret Haubert. She had promised that she would stay in her childhood home as long as she was needed. She kept her promise; when her mother died (within a year of her marriage), she followed her husband to a new life in England in 1893, at the age of 21.

Alice Marie and Gaston had six children: Renée, Georges, Jeanne, Alfred, Henri and Alice. They lived in the East End of London and their mother never mastered the English language; their father insisted that only French was to be spoken in the home. My mother, Renée, was the eldest child and did not learn English until she went to school. She then taught her brothers and sisters so that they would not have the same problems she had understanding her classes. Their mother was Catholic but their father was not interested in religion and was known to have ordered visiting nuns to leave their home. They did not have much money and for years they lived in a community with other French people in the East End of London.

Later they moved to a larger house in a better district, the suburb of Walthamstow in North London. Her father drew intricate drawings for his carving patterns and also painted beautiful detailed maps of England and France that hung on the walls of their home. Sadly, no one seems to know what became of them. Alice Marie lived in the house (until her death in 1951) with her youngest daughter, Alice, who probably sold them when she had to move to a smaller house. Gaston made lovely furniture, carved with beautiful details, some of which ended up years later in our home in Bexleyheath.

Most of the children in the family were very artistic. They designed and sewed clothes, made fancy hats for society ladies, painted pictures, drew maps and made woodcarvings. They had no indoor plumbing or hot water in the home. They only had outside toilets, used oil lamps for light and cooked on a coal stove. Improvements did not come until the late 1930s or after. My grandmother stayed home and looked after her family, grew flowers and herbs in her garden and kept a 'pot au feu,' a stock pot simmering in French style on the back of the stove that provided a warm hearth for her several cats to sleep near. When she went shopping, she pointed at whatever she wanted to buy; her English was not understandable to the cockney (East London) shopkeepers in the market.

When Renée was 21, she married the boy next door, Second Lieutenant Albert Derbyshire, who had joined the army together with her brother Georges. Albert was later killed at the Battle of the Somme in France in 1917. His remains were never found and I have seen his name on the Arras Memorial in Pas de Calais, Northern France. I know that when I was young she would wonder whether there was a possibility that he was still alive . . . among those who were too mangled to ever return to their families. We knew there were hospitals in England caring for such casualties. I know she often thought of him.

As a young girl, she was very fond of her father and was devastated when he was hospitalized and died in the same year, just as her soldier husband. For several years after the war, she lived with friends and worked as a secretary in London. Her sisters did not know any details of her life at that time; she never mentioned it.

About five years after her husband's death, my mother and father met in 1922 when they were both working for Hatry's Jeweler in London. Mother worked there first as a Pitman-style shorthand typist before catching the unwanted interest of the boss' son. When my father, William James Beaver, was hired as a Hatry's clerk, she became friends with him. This annoyed the boss and caused them both to be fired. It was probably a good thing as Clarence Hatry, the owner, was later arrested and jailed for forgery and swindling the British public of the equivalent of nearly $10,000,000 by borrowing money on forged municipal bonds.

In 1929, he was sentenced to 14 years in prison. "He is remembered by fellow jewelers as the sallow, baldish, unhealthy looking little man who bought $2,500,000 worth of jewelry for his wife, pawned it and redeemed it again and again as he traversed a career as full of ups and downs as a picket fence." (Quoted from a Time magazine article dated: October 21, 1929)

Mother and Daddy, whom she called 'Jack' (army nickname) while his family called him Will, were married in October 1923. They lived with his mother, my Granny Beaver, in a house in Sidcup, Kent. Mother got a job tailoring. She was an excellent seamstress and sewed beautifully all her life, often by hand with the tiniest of stitches. Many years later, she told me that by wearing tight corsets she was able to work almost up until my birth. This was an age when expectant mothers were supposed to stay home quietly, hidden until their child was born. However, she thought working caused problems in the end. Even though I was a very small baby, I had to be delivered with forceps and she was very ill for several days.

Daddy had various jobs for years, working as an insurance salesman, sweet shop owner, and office clerk until the middle of the thirties. Then he became a dairy inspector with Express Dairies in Old Bexley, checking the routes of delivery men on a horse-drawn cart and sometimes over-seeing the bottling plant. He was with them until he died in 1941 at age 45.

He had been in the army, having enlisted on March 22, 1915, and had fought in the trenches of France with the Royal Fusiliers during the Battles of the Somme and Ypres. Later, after being wounded twice (once when a bullet shattered his knee), he was transferred to the Royal Army Ordnance Corps. He had been severely gassed in the trenches, leaving him with lung problems for the rest of his short life. He was in the Egyptian Expeditionary Forces until he left the army on February 29, 1920. As far as I know, he never received any pension or disablement compensation.

Returning soldiers were unable to find jobs or housing for their families. Men had a hard time making a living after coming from the mud and fighting in the trenches in France. Although the Allies were winners, it had been a devastating war. Being thought of as heroes did not impress them; it didn't pay the rent! With her second husband being ill and unable to work a lot of the time, Mother had the fear of war and poverty that was prevalent in many wives and mothers during the years of depression between the two world wars. As my father had spent time in Egypt during his army service, he would have enjoyed living in a warmer climate but my mother would not consider moving overseas as he would have liked.

Mother was 31 and Daddy 29 when I was born on August 17, 1925 in the home of Elizabeth Carter Beaver, my paternal grandmother, and I was named Joy Alicia by my mother's sister, Jeanne. My mother had a difficult labor and was disappointed to have a daughter. In those days it was important to have a son first to carry on the family name; she was never hesitant to tell me this. I grew so used to hearing it that it did not matter.

My grandparents had legally separated in 1919, and my Granny lived in the house with only the youngest of her six children, Winifred, who was 12 at the time. Mother had quit working by then but I understand that father was still taking the train to the City of London each day to work, a 30-minute ride from Sidcup station to London Bridge station on the Southern Railway. I can just imagine him with a bowler hat and a rolled umbrella running for the 7:32 a.m. train to buy a low-priced workman's ticket to his job as an insurance agent; the later trains cost more.

My parents started to buy a house a couple of years later but were unable to handle the costs with fathers' disabilities and inability to work full time. It was a brand new, modern house around the corner from Granny Beaver's house. My brother Tony (Anthony Gaston) was born there in 1928 and during that time my parents were operating a sweet shop close by. I remember nothing about that house but stories have been handed down through the years. Mother, Grandma and Auntie Alice tell me that one day Tony's little clothes were hung on the fireguard to warm so they would be nice and cozy for him after his bath. He was in his pram and I was in the room alone with him for just a minute. By the time my mother and aunt returned, I had thrown all his clothes into the fire and was trying to get him out of the pram and throw him in, too. I accept this as a family story but believe I always enjoyed having Tony as my brother.

The 1930s were an age of innocence for children. They were told very little of life or anything of importance and problems were never discussed in their hearing. Love was not something that was talked about in those days. People didn't say, "I love you" or hug and kiss their children constantly as they did later in the century. Yet, Tony and I knew we were safe and cared for. Daddy told me that loving someone was something special, private and between two people. For instance, the word 'Darling' was only for that special person. In playing, I called Tony 'darling' and Daddy heard me. I can see him now standing by the kitchen window, asking me not to call anyone darling until I was old enough to understand how to use the word properly.

Tony was a favorite child with everyone, especially our mother; he was the son for whom she had planned. With his fair hair, cheeky little smile, intelligent and mischievous ways, he was well loved and a joyous, golden child. I thought he was wonderful and could do anything.

We had a lovely large house and garden in which to grow up. We had moved into a rental house called 'Ringwood' at 137 Sidcup Hill, Sidcup, Kent in late 1928. It was a charmer, over 100 years old with sand-colored brick. It had two stories and was a semi- detached house covered with bright colorful leaves of Virginia creeper with a side porch entrance.

The front door opened into a large entrance hall with an impressive staircase, a large living room across the front, a dining room with windows overlooking the garden and a spacious kitchen. Upstairs were four bedrooms, a bathroom and a separate toilet which was an interesting high-ceilinged room about six-foot square. The highlight of the room was the smooth, beautifully polished mahogany wood seat about two feet wide that went from wall to wall. There was also an overhead tank and a chain hanging down for flushing. There was a beautiful staircase with a polished wooden handrail with a curving 'U' shape, leading to a large landing where Tony could play with his toy soldiers and I with my double-jointed, porcelain head dolls with eyes that closed and real hair.

Playing in the Lupines ~ 1931

The house had gas lighting, little lamps on the walls with a white mantle inside that had to be lit with a match. They made a dancing flame that threw strange shadows around the room. Our parents slept at one end of the large front bedroom and Tony and I slept at the other. The other bedrooms were rented out to lodgers, politely called 'paying guests;' we had a lady helping Mother with the housekeeping and cooking. Mr. Mawhood and Mr. deBruin were steady renters for years. Mr. Mawhood was a big quiet man, perhaps an office worker. I know he caught the train to London every day and was friendly with all the family. Mr. deBruin was a member of the brown shirts (Nazi Party followers) and I remember him as a short, strutting, arrogant little man with black hair. He would rush off in the evenings to attend his meetings and return very late. He was different; nobody realized at the time (early 1930s) how serious and troublesome the 'dark' politics of Europe were becoming. Though he stayed a long time, Mother didn't like him. He didn't like children but Daddy just thought he was funny and amusing.

Ringwood has long stayed in my memory; a home with a fireplace in all main rooms upstairs and down with large windows and high ceilings. We lived mainly in the kitchen with a coal fire burning in the cool weather and a large mahogany table in the center of the room, where we had our meals and played board games like snakes and ladders or did jigsaw puzzles. We had a wooden puzzle with a picture of the two royal princesses, Elizabeth and Margaret Rose. Their whole faces were on large pieces and we would compete to get them as starters for our section. Daddy always sat at the far side of the table where he could look out into the back garden. The cooking and dishwashing was done in a scullery off the main area. In the scullery, there was a bricked-in area surrounding a large, built-in copper tub with a gas burner beneath, used for boiling the laundry that was always done on Monday and pegged on an outside clothes line to dry. Tuesday was ironing day and the room would become full of steam and the smell of the soap. So often the door from the scullery was left open, no matter what the weather.

Tony and Joy picking gooseberries ~ 1931

The scullery door opened onto a very large back garden, full of fruit trees, gooseberry and raspberry bushes, rhubarb plants but no vegetables. There were lawns, flowers and overgrown areas. We could play there but were not to eat the fruit. Interestingly, there is a picture of Tony with a mouthful of gooseberries and I remember biting into a pear that had a wasp in it and getting badly stung. Perhaps we didn't listen very well.

Sometimes relatives would come to visit in the summer and a table would be set up outside for tea and a net for badminton. But mostly, we children had it to ourselves. A path sloped down away from the house and we used an old doll's pram for a scooter. Way out back was a wheat field and a tumbledown shed belonging to a neighboring farmer. In there, we used old saucepans we found to make mud pies (a forbidden game) that got us into trouble. One year we ran through the wheat growing tall at the edge of the field and smashed it down just before harvest time when you could hide in it. We were terrified when the angry farmer shouted at our mother about her naughty children destroying his crop; after that we stayed out of his sight.

My brother and I had so much space to play inside and out. We were always together in those early years, inseparable with no other playmates. I was very happy in this house and it has always been in my memory. In the early 1980s, I was visiting my Uncle Jack who still lived in Sidcup and he wanted to take me to see the house again. We rode the bus down Sidcup Hill and got off at the proper stop but, unbelievably, there was no house there! It had been torn down and some flats had been built. The Foots Cray Baptist Church next door that we had attended was still there but my dream house was no more!

As children, Tony and I went to the same school, Sidcup Hill Primary in Oxford Road. We usually walked together and sometimes Mother came with us. After age 11 (much later), we went to all boys or all girls schools, Walking up the hill to school each day we passed a private school for boys. They wore bright red schoolboy caps, short grey flannel trousers (as did all school boys through age of 11), white shirts and ties and played in the schoolyard in front of the school. Tony and his mates would shout and rile up the red caps. They wanted to fight but were confined to their schoolyard and were not allowed out.

Tony and I did the shopping together and there were no supermarkets then. From the time I was about seven, we went to the butcher's, grocers, greengrocers and fish shop, all small, locally-owned businesses further up Sidcup Hill. Mother did not go out very much as she was not in very good health, although she lived to be 84 years old. Father was either working or resting as he had significant trouble breathing; everything was an effort for him.

Sidcup Hill was the main street going through the shopping district; by the time it passed our house, it was more of a rural street. In fact, sometimes a steamroller would work on it so maybe it wasn't properly paved. I was young and didn't pay attention to things like that. I do remember an accident when the steamroller hit a boy on a bicycle and the ambulance came and took him away.

When we first moved in, there were open fields across the road from us. But soon there was a lot of activity. Middleton Avenue was built and a new housing estate popped up. We weren't in the countryside anymore. There were very few cars in those days; in fact, in all my 22 years in England I only rode in a car about six times. I only knew a few people who had a car or could drive. We were able to get anywhere for just pennies on public buses, trams or trains.

About November 1933, Tony caught the measles. He was in bed for days in the big front bedroom with the curtains drawn to keep the light from damaging his eyes and the door closed to keep me out, but I didn't stay out. Two weeks later, Tony was back in school and I was sick and had to sit outside the classroom until Mother came for me. The doctor came to the house and diagnosed scarlet fever and sent for an ambulance. I was taken to the fever hospital right before Christmas to stay for six weeks. After spending most of that time in bed in a big ward full of children, I remember being dressed in my hat and coat and waiting with some others for the ambulance to take us home. When the doctor gave me my final examination, he said I had scarlet fever again and was put back to bed for another six weeks.

After lying in bed for so long, my legs were shaky and I found it difficult to walk. My mother had taught me to knit when I was about four and she sent me some wool and needles (although the wool got terribly tangled and I remember more about untangling instead of knitting). It was Easter before I returned home. I was hoping to get my Christmas presents but I learned in those days that when people with fevers were put in hospital, the house had to be quarantined and fumigated, as well as the toys and dolls burned to stop the illness from spreading. Our toy cupboard at the bottom of a big Welsh dresser was almost empty. I was disappointed but happy to be home. We had a pantry that was off the kitchen, in a cupboard under the stairs. It was dark and we were allowed to play in there with a few new toys. A popular song at that time was 'The Isle of Capri,' which I learned from listening to the nurses' wireless (radio) at the hospital. I sang it night and day at home to the annoyance of my parents; I think I was just pleased to be home.

Every Sunday we were sent to Sunday school at the Foots Cray Baptist Church next door (we lived behind these trees on the very left, by the drain pipe). Tony and I had both been christened in the Church of England although that was too far to walk every Sunday morning.

Foots Cray Baptist Church, Sidcup Hill

As I remember, we also went to Brownie and Cub Scout meetings at that church. My memory of Sunday school is vague yet I do remember a couple of Sunday school treats or outings. We were taken to the seaside, probably Southend or Sheerness. Though more popular, the towns of Margate or Ramsgate further along the Kentish coast would have been considered too far for a group of young children on a coach trip without their parents and only a few teachers.

Little girls in those days wore pretty dresses; trousers and shorts for women did not come into style until the 1940s wartime. Anyway, there I was in my pretty dress with my sandals standing on the edge of the sea; I was happy. Nobody told me about the tide and as I stood there, the water came around my feet. As it receded, the sand shifted and I went down. The teacher helped me up and tried to dry off my soaked, sand-covered dress. Poor teacher; within minutes I fell again. Tony tried to ignore his soaking wet sister as I was an embarrassment to him.

Another Sunday school outing was to a place (maybe by the sea) that had a grassy field, nearby where an old rusty, open-top car was discarded. All the boys were fascinated and wanted to try to drive it. They pried open the door and some of them climbed in. Tony was still on the outside and when the door was slammed; his hand was in it. Yells, blood, tears, excuses; the group was in an uproar. Who cared for his hand I don't know: a doctor, the cottage hospital or the teacher? All I know was that Tony had a nasty wound and a scar for the rest of his life. I can't remember any other outings, but maybe by then the Beaver children were no longer invited.

It was not until I was much older that I realized we did not have much money for extras. I was accustomed to my mother sewing her clothes and mine from Auntie Alice's hand-me-downs. She also made Tony's clothes. We always had enough to eat but not many toys and certainly no holidays away from home as some families did. Our parents made our lives happy and we were not aware of being deprived in any way.

I'm sure now that our parents loved each other and us but their life in the 1920s and 1930s was hard. Ill health and lack of jobs and money made their everyday life difficult. Daddy was a very quiet man who was kind and gentle with his family. I never saw him angry or heard him raise his voice. He called our mother, 'Pet' or 'Wren' and sang to her 'Roses of Picardy,' a popular song from the Great War.

Daddy's stories of his youth and the war kept us excited and laughing as we sat on the floor beside his chair listening to him. He grew up in the East End of London where his father, my grandfather, William Thomas Beaver, was a Metropolitan policeman. His beat was around and inside the Tower of London grounds.

Daddy lived in a terraced house on Tower Hill, houses that were razed years before to build a tourist shopping area that sold souvenirs, flags and ice cream cones. He and his brothers spent a lot of time roaming the East End, home of the London Cockney. His father was born within the sound of Bow Bells (a requisite for a cockney) although he said he was not a proper cockney. I don't know why, maybe not the correct ancestors. They played tricks and got into all kinds of mischief.

Tower of London

Most of the houses in the East End of London were referred to as 'terraced,' a row of several houses joined together where the front doors were in pairs, side-by-side. The boys would tie the front door knob of one house to the door knob of the next with a piece of rope, ring both door bells and run away. Nobody could open their door as it was tied to the neighbors and they would each be pulling against the other. Another trick was to tie a string from a lamp post to the front gate about the height of a man. In the darkness, the hat of a person walking by would be knocked to the ground.

Daddy's stories of the Great War (1914-1918), his service in the trenches, and then later in Egypt, always fascinated Tony and me. He was in France for most of the war and must have seen some horrendous episodes in his years there, though he never spoke of the actual fighting or death.

He said they dug trenches often in deep mud, did a lot of marching and never had enough to eat. He spent time in hospitals as he had been injured in the legs and had no right kneecap; the bones were wired together so that he could walk. He would encourage us to touch it and it was all soft with no bone. He told of the visits between the allies and the Germans at Christmastime, singing carols across from each other in the trenches and the comradeship between both sides. But the next day they were shooting at each other again and crawling in the mud and barbed wire in the trenches. He told us that when they came home on leave from France, they were so filthy and covered in mud and lice that their mother insisted they take off all their clothes and scrub themselves in the back garden before coming into the house.

Daddy would sing all the wartime songs: 'There's a Long, Long Trail A-Winding,' 'Pack Up Your Troubles' and 'It's a Long Way to Tipperary.' I remember a lot of the words of those songs until this day! He spoke of being stationed in Egypt late in the war—how warm it was there and not any fighting (by then, an army of occupation). He told us how he shot an alligator there; I still have a bag made from its skin. He always rode a bicycle in my childhood years. He rode it everywhere—to work, to see family or shop. When he wasn't riding it, he was working on it. He would take it apart, hang the parts on the washing line with string and paint them. He never drove a car.

Mother was a more nervous person. She was in the cottage hospital up Sidcup Hill several times but as children we were not told why. She enjoyed her own company and did not mix much with the neighbors or like going shopping. She taught me how to knit and sew; I think she taught Tony too. I remember him knitting a scarf. I knitted a doll's outfit once and entered it in a child's competition sponsored by a newspaper and was very disappointed when I did not win a prize—I was only told how to remedy my mistakes.

She, too, would talk about her childhood, her father's artistic work and her family link to France. She once went to Paris with her father to see her grandmother, but that sadly was her only visit there.

Mother was very proud of her French ancestry and was quite sad that she had not been born in France. She was raised a Catholic and in her old age took religious classes to renew her faith and French language lessons. She was very intellectual, believed in a good education and gracious manners for her children and read a great deal. Napoleon was her hero as he is with all Frenchmen; he was their Emperor.

Her house was always clean and tidy, her cooking was average but with the depression and the war, she did well with what was available to her on the market. Though she was often nervous and distressed, she took good care of her family.

I never traveled much as a child, only trips across London to see my maternal 'French' grandmother in Walthamstow, East London, or Auntie Jeanne (my mother's sister) in Streatham, South East London. These were seemingly long trips requiring both bus and train journeys. Tony and I loved to go visiting though we were often expected to play outside. Both of our grandmothers had cats, which we teased unmercifully.

One grandma raised chickens, which were a bore though they could be disturbed easily and get noisy. Our Grandma Therin spoke with a French accent; in over 50 years in England she never really mastered the English language. When I started to learn French in school, I tried to speak to her in French. She said I would never learn; I had too much of an English accent and did not have the musical tone of the French language.

Tony did much better and I always believed that he took after the Therin family. He was more careful, clever and more able to do intricate things; he always had a charm about him that our French relatives also had, whereas I was always clumsy and not too coordinated. Grandma Therin was small, always wore black or gray (never color) long skirts, fixed her hair in a bun and was quite strict. There would be family dinner parties at her house at 21 Lloyd Road, Walthamstow—quiet and sedate. One thing we dearly loved that was so special at her house was a wind-up gramophone with a big horn on it in the front drawing room. It looked like the gramophone in the ad, 'His Master's Voice.' We listened to opera, classical music and Enrico Caruso singing. As children we were allowed to have wine (diluted with lemonade) with our meal—a special privilege!

In the Sidcup garden with Grandma Therin ~ 1931

About 1933, mother's brother, Uncle Georges (who was now an engineer with a big company in the North of England) got married to Ada Pinson. I believe he had lived at home all his life with his mother and sister, Alice, except when he was in the army during the war. I think his mother relied on him and was not happy that he was getting married. In fact, she did not speak to him for about 14 years—until they met again at his sister Jeanne's funeral. Tony and I were not told about this rift but in the quiet way of listening children; we learned a lot without ever questioning. We were all dressed up—I even had white gloves to wear to the wedding. After their marriage, Georges and Ada lived on Faraday Avenue in Blackfen, within walking distance of our house.

Later they had two sons, Bernard and Brian, and our mother would take us to visit sometimes.

Our Granny Beaver lived in Sidcup and we could walk to her house and to the house of our Aunt Bessie, Uncle Jack and cousins (Joan and Betty) who lived across the street from her at 40, Bedford Road. We would go there sometimes on Sunday afternoons, riding the bus if it was bad weather. Granny Beaver was a big woman who hardly moved from her chair. She was kind, soft and scented and we loved her. But our mother did not get along well with her. She felt that Granny was not a respectable woman as her husband had left her. They had separated when he retired from the Metropolitan Police Force in 1919 and he lived at Cliftonville on the coast of Kent. Father was one of six children and when we went to Sidcup, there were several aunts, uncles, and cousins (Joan and Betty); everyone was always laughing and joking.

On October 16, 1934, we went to school in the morning and when we came home in the afternoon a strange lady opened the door and told us we had a new baby brother! Geoffrey James had joined our family. In the innocence of children in those days, I at least, had no idea there was to be a baby and of course, we were never told. It would be too embarrassing to Mummy, although Mummy did say much later that Tony had told her that she was getting to be like a big fat bear. I have been told that I said to the lady at the door that I didn't need a brother as I already had one. I guess I didn't think brothers were a good idea! I really can't remember how I felt but I do remember my responsibilities were greater.

Geoffrey's arrival made a big change in my life. As big sister, I could take him for rides in his pram; feed him his bottle of 'Cow and Gate' baby formula; play with him on the rug; knit little clothes, booties and matinee jackets for him and try to keep him quiet even when Tony teased him! Shopping was easier too because I could put the goods in the pram instead of carrying them in a basket. In those days you could safely leave the baby in the pram (with its brake on) outside the store while you shopped.

After several years, the paying guests had moved away and after Geoffrey was born, Tony and I were moved to a different bedroom. At Christmas that year, we hung our stockings at the end of our beds and I received a suede leather bag to carry my knitting in from Father Christmas. Until we moved to our next house, it was the only year I remember celebrating Christmas and having a big decorated Christmas tree in the dining room.

In the spring of 1935, we moved to a more modern and much smaller house in Bexleyheath. While several miles away, it was closer to the job Daddy now had as a dairy inspector for Express Dairies in Old Bexley, a small village a couple of miles from our new home. This house was not as much fun; no hiding places and the small back garden was in full view of the kitchen and living room windows so we were more closely watched. We were growing up: new responsibilities, new schools, family losses and drastic changes.

And trouble was brewing in Germany with a new dictator and his entourage.

Chapter Two

GROWING UP IN BEXLEYHEATH

Our story continues but there are many changes—a new baby brother and a new home. Though Tony and I continued to do many things together, as we got older we made friends in school, went to a different Sunday school and did more things with the Girl Guides and Boy Scouts—sharing with more outsiders.

Geoffrey was becoming a more active member in our games though, as with any younger brother, not always as welcome as he would like to be. I remember him with affection and know I took him to a lot of places with me.

Moving to Bexleyheath in 1935 seemed to cause lots of changes in our lives; I was almost ten, Tony seven and Geoffrey only five months old. For the first few months we went to Brampton Road School, about a ten-minute walk away. I know I went there but I don't remember much about the school. We walked to the end of Marlborough Road (our street) right onto Brampton Road and straight ahead over the curved, brick-built bridge with the railway running beneath it.

We could go to the other end of our street and over the level crossing in Gypsy Road, which seemed a lot more daring to us. We'd jump and dance around as if we were thrilled by the thought of a train passing. The rails were for electric trains although the live rails stopped short each side of the crossing. So we really weren't in any danger but we had to play as if we were. After we'd been there a few years they built a steel girder bridge over the level crossing, which took some of the thrill away.

Marlborough Road

At 47 Marlborough Road I had my own bedroom, a small room over the front entrance hall. Mummy and Daddy were in the big front bedroom and Tony and Geoffrey in the back. Tony was always trying science experiments in that room. He had the edges of the dresser burned and all the finish stripped off the top with his science experiments; he was determined to be a scientist. Poor Mummy, no wonder she had headaches! The bathroom was upstairs too, with the pipes running down the outside of the wall. We soon found that outside plumbing caused frozen pipes in the bathroom every winter. I find it strange that many English houses are still built the same way; it was quite an uncomfortable situation! We'd take up kettles of water so we could wash but be unable to have a bath or to flush the toilet. For some reason there was a hole high in the bathroom wall that let in the outside cold air in for ventilation. All new houses had one but it made the bathroom very cold.

Downstairs we had a sitting room in front (in which we never sat, unless we had visitors) that had a big bay window, a couple of upholstered chairs and a sideboard but not much else. We lived in the dining room that had glass French doors opening into the back garden. We had a big round mahogany table with dining chairs and a leather armchair each side of the fireplace. We had an 'antique' floral carpet that Mummy always called her 'Brussels,' (the name of a very valuable carpet). Both downstairs rooms had fireplaces angled across the inside corner, as did the two main bedrooms upstairs and all leading to a central chimney.

It was a semi-detached house and the neighbor's was the same, although a reversed floor plan and all chimneys were in the center of the roofs. The hot water tank was behind the dining room fireplace; so to have hot water we had to light the coal fire. It was a newly-built house with white stucco on the outside, part of S. H. Alabaster's new modern housing estate. In the 1940s, a man came round for the rent every week (always on Monday) collecting seven shillings and sixpence. The exchange rate at that time was $5 to the English pound making the rent about $2 per week. Wages were very low compared with today's standards. When I started work in December 1941, I was making 25 shillings per week (20 shillings equaled one English pound)!

Mummy must have known for sometime that we were going to move as she had started some cuttings from the Sidcup Hill privet hedge. By the time we moved in, they had rooted. She planted them in a row across the garden, a few feet away from the back of the house. They grew rapidly and we soon had a hedge giving privacy to our downstairs rooms.

Joy and Tony with berries from the garden ~ 1931

The clothesline was inside this small paved area (useful for hanging Daddy's bicycle parts to be painted) as was the coal shed. The coal man would carry hundredweight sacks of coal (114 pounds per English hundredweight) over his shoulder, round through the side gate and then dump them in the top opening of the coal shed. We would then gather coal from a small opening in the bottom and fill the coalscuttle to take into the house and place by the fireplace for adding to the fire.

It was also the scene of a nasty accident. Tony, now about ten years old, had been asked to chop some firewood. Geoffrey, always interested in whatever was going on, followed him outside. Tony started chopping and Geoffrey (still a toddler) moved in closer. Tony raised the axe and caught Geoffrey on the left temple. Talk about pandemonium—Mummy was hysterical! Geoffrey's head was badly bleeding. He was bawling and running his fingers through the blood, spreading it all over himself. All Tony could say was, "Well, it was the wrong side of the axe!!" We managed to get Geoffrey cleaned up. He did have a big 'egg' on his head but recovered well. Mummy quieted down although it was upsetting to her for a long time; she worried about her baby. Poor lady, her children were always causing some kind of a crisis! Once, when she was disciplining us outside and had left a hot iron on the wooden kitchen table, it scorched the whole corner of the table. Luckily, it was just an old-fashioned type iron that was heated on the gas stove.

This house had a very uninteresting back garden with no trees. There was grass but it certainly could never be called a lawn. We used to dig big holes in it, probably in an attempt to dig through to Australia! We were told that if it were possible to dig through the earth, we would end up in Australia. So, we tried. One time we pitched a tent outside. It might have been one of Tony's Cub Scout projects. We children wanted to sleep out there but Mother said no. I think Daddy tried to grow a few vegetables when we first moved there but I don't remember them being much of a success. The front garden was very narrow; it had a rock wall between it and the pavement (sidewalk) and I can't remember any flowers.

Mother enjoyed being out in the back garden late at night whenever there was a thunder and lightning storm or heavy rain. She would quietly stand there, often for long periods of time, bundled up in a big coat but no hat or umbrella. We could see her silhouetted out there as the lightning flashed. She stood there often in the dark during the war when we could see the smoke and flames of London burning during the incendiary raids of the German bombers, about 12 miles away.

She stood there for hours on one night in November 1936 when the Crystal Palace in Sydenham, a town between London and Bexleyheath, burned to the ground. Sir Joseph Paxton originally designed the Crystal

Palace from an idea of Albert, Prince Consort of Queen Victoria. It was a massive iron girder exhibition hall totally covered in glass, like a big conservatory with a domed roof built in Hyde Park, London. The exhibition of industry and science was opened in 1851 and was a tremendous success. People came from all parts of Europe and the British Colonies—exhibiting their new inventions and discoveries as well as visiting the show. After the Great Exhibition was closed, the Crystal Palace building was moved to Sydenham Hill in South London and became a sports centre with football, car racing, cricket and many other sports. Since the large glass palace burned that November night, it has been a sports centre and continues to be the key element of the park. England was a pioneer in television and the first company was established at Crystal Palace, June 1934. In 1937, color television was demonstrated but, with the arrival of the war in 1939, was stopped in favor of other needed defense inventions.

Early in 1936, a policeman came on his bicycle to our house in the middle of the night. As I slept in the room over the front door, I heard him knock. It was uncanny; I knew immediately that he had come because our Granny Beaver had died. It turned out to be true and Daddy went cycling off into the night with him.

We missed our Granny. After she died, Auntie Winnie (who had lived with her) came to stay with us for a few years and some of Granny's furniture was moved to our house. There was a beautiful, light oak, Welsh dresser with dark wood inserts and large mirrors; I believe someone in the family had built it. It was put in our dining room and held dishes, cutlery as well as brandy and Scotch whiskey 'for medicinal use.'

Auntie Winnie eventually went to nursing school and was a nurse during World War II and later served as a matron at a boy's school overseas in Kenya. After the war I did not see her for years; I finally located her. In 1984, on our way to South Africa to visit with my brother Tony, Carl and I with our daughters, Vivian and Barbara accompanied by her son, Ryan, had lunch with Winnie in London. She never married, had been in a bad accident in Kenya and had to wear orthopedic boots. Amazingly, she was just as I had remembered her.

Every year, we would get some frog spawn from a stream or a lake nearby and Mummy had a large glass bowl she put in the middle of this dresser. So we watched the tadpoles develop; the whole family was

interested. One year, about 1941, we got great big frog spawn that developed into big tadpoles. We were all curious about the difference until
tiny toads started to evolve. Once matured, we usually put them outside.
But on one occasion, we forgot. One night we went to bed with five
or six toads in the bowl; when we got up the next morning, the bowl
was empty—no toads!! We searched high and low, but never did find
them, not even in our beds!! Everyone was suspect, but nobody admitted
anything. I know I had no hand in the disappearance and Mother was
quite upset. I think she had enjoyed watching them.

As Tony and I grew older we thought that calling our mother 'Mummy' was too babyish. We tried Mother or Mater, too pompous! We were
both learning French in school so Tony suggested 'Maman' (French for
mother, the final 'n' is silent). This worked well for a long time and
gradually developed into 'Ma;' that's what we called her for the rest of
her days. She seemed quite happy with it. Daddy was always 'Daddy.'

Daddy's father, William Thomas Beaver, now lived right on the coast
of Kent; the sea lapped the end of his backyard. He had moved there
about 1935 or 1936. Daddy went down there for several days during the
summer to help him move to that house. While he was there, Daddy
wrote some lovely letters to our mother that I treasure to this day. Later,
the whole family went to stay at Grandpa's home for our first holiday by
the sea; I think we traveled by coach. Geoffrey was probably almost four
by then. He was a chubby little boy at that time and there are pictures
of him playing happily in the sand in his 'monogrammed' bathing suit.
Grandpa had a nice two-story house plus a guest cottage where Daddy
and Mummy stayed. Tony and I slept in the main house in one of the
bedrooms upstairs. The ceiling was slanted and the windows close to
the floor. We could hang way out from them, as I remember, a little
dangerously!

Ma was not very comfortable there as Grandpa had a housekeeper,
Mrs. Clara Peel. Ma felt Mrs. Peel was too demanding, too familiar and
far too friendly with Grandpa. I think we may have returned home earlier
than planned. I know Ma was really unhappy but Daddy was pleased to
be with his father as they had not spent much time together in recent
years.

It was amusing that every time he took a picture of his father it was out of focus; his father's head was cut off in the picture! It became a family joke!

Grandpa Beaver, Mrs. Peel, Ma, Tony, Joy with Geoffrey in front ~ 1936-37

Tony and I enjoyed ourselves on the beach and in the garden, especially since it was right next door to Manston Airport and there were lots of little planes flying around. Mrs. Peel spent a lot of time in her vegetable garden and she cooked our meals. As I recall, Tony and I thought she was very old!

Daddy and Grandpa took Tony and me to visit a lady in Cliftonville, a nearby resort town on the English Channel. I can remember a very big lady opening the door, appearing in a voluminous floor-length black dress with her gray hair in a big poufy bun. Grandpa said she was our Great Aunt Maria, his sister. Years later, when I visited 90-year-old Auntie Bessie in Sidcup, she denied that Grandpa had a sister! When studying genealogy recently, I read in his will a bequest naming 'his sister, Maria;' I think Bessie had forgotten. We were introduced to her but I don't believe we went into the house that day with Grandpa; I can only see her framed by the ornate door. Maybe she didn't want children inside or maybe it was not her home and she was a housekeeper there.

1935 saw lots of celebrations in England as King George V and Queen Mary had been on the throne for 25 years. In the schools, all children were given commemorative mugs and blue-linen covered books about the history of their reign. In the summer there were street parties and firework displays in the towns and villages, as well as memorable royal parades in London. In Danson Park one evening, only ten minutes' walk from our house, we went to stand in the open area to watch the fireworks, which were displayed on the far side of a lake. Geoffrey was in his pram with the hood up, supposedly asleep. Daddy had bought a newspaper and put it in the pram. Apparently, Geoffrey found it and chewed it all up. His face was all black with newsprint but he was quiet during the fireworks! The event had a fantastic finale, ending with silhouettes of the Royal couple outlined with fireworks.

At the end of 1935, King George V became ill and he died in January 1936. Lots of people wore black armbands in his memory and the whole country was in mourning for he was well-liked. His widow, then known as the Dowager Queen Mary, was a tall, elegant lady, always beautifully dressed but no longer seen as often in public. On the King's death, Edward, the Prince of Wales became King Edward VIII. But it was a sad year for him and for the British public. The British people have a great affection for their royalty and, as Prince of Wales, he had been very popular. Things changed when, as King, he wanted to marry his lady-friend, Mrs. Wallis Warfield Simpson and make her Queen. She was a twice divorced American, who had two living husbands and did not meet the approval of the British government or the Church of England that did not recognize divorce.

So, he lost their support.

After many months of pressure to give her up, he finally renounced the throne. I remember well the dark December day when he spoke on the radio and announced his abdication, leaving England in favor of his brother, who became King George VI. As I came home from school on the trolley bus, the newsboys were yelling out the latest developments and people on the bus were crying because we were losing our King. He had been a favorite with the 'man in the street.' Daddy used to cycle to work in the dark early morning hours and told us that Edward VIII's procession of cars passed him on his way to work that day; the former king was leaving his country for the rest of his life. At that time the general public did not realize the rising problems in Europe. Hitler's power was increasing swiftly and many in the government saw real trouble on the horizon. Edward VIII and Mrs. Simpson were inclined to be friendly with Hitler and the German government. This was a problem for British Prime Minister, Stanley Baldwin, and members of Parliament and became an added reason to request Edward's abdication.

Lots of preparations had been made for celebrating King Edward VIII coronation in May 1937. But as he gave up the throne, moved to France and married Mrs. Simpson, they were given the title of the Duke and Duchess of Windsor and, except for a period during the war when he was governor of Bermuda, Edward lived in France for the rest of his days.

The celebrations were reorganized for King George VI, his younger brother, and were held on the day originally planned for King Edward VIII, May 12, 1937. Although the English people thought of George VI as a very shy man who stuttered, they accepted him graciously. He won a place in their respect in the years that followed. Once again there was lots of excitement. Commemorative books and mugs were given to us in school and there were street parties, firework displays and parades in Central London. Daddy took Tony and me on the train to join the large crowds of happy people standing in front of Buckingham Palace to see the newly-crowned King George VI and Queen Elizabeth come out on the balcony. We waited for hours in the crowd but they didn't appear and we had to catch the last train back to Bexleyheath. Later we learned that they appeared after midnight; by then we were on our way home. I remember it being an exciting time though!

Daddy took us to London several times and taught me to love London; the cathedrals and churches—Westminster Abbey, Buckingham Palace, and The Tower of London. We went up a tight medieval, circular stone staircase in the Tower to see the Crown Jewels. When we were fairly little he took pictures of Tony and me sitting by the lions at the base of Nelson's Column in Trafalgar Square.

Joy and Tony by the lions of Trafalgar Square ~ 1933

He also took us to Regents Park Zoo where we rode on elephants and camels. We also watched the chimpanzees' tea party—monkeys sitting at a table with cups, saucers and a teapot, acting like rowdy grown-ups. They were so funny.

I think I got my love of history from him, though Ma enjoyed London and history too. She was very intellectual and well read and Napoleon was one of the famous people she liked to read about. Along with European history, she also read 'War and Peace,' 'Anna Karenina,' and other books of Leo Tolstoy, a Russian author of the late 19th century. Ma spent a lot of time reading, listening to book readings and plays on the radio. I think she preferred to do that rather than anything else, except knitting and sewing. It was not until later, after Daddy died, that she started to go out more. Both Daddy and Ma taught us a lot of history and geography; they took us to the library every week and encouraged us to read.

On Christmas Eve, for about three years in a row, Daddy took us on the trolley bus to Woolwich Market to buy for Christmas day. He always carried a big sack over his shoulder and the first stop he made was at the 'cockles and whelk' stall in the open market to buy a pint of whelks (a shellfish). They came in a tin mug with a pin. There was a round black membrane that was discarded first. Then the whelk was unwound from its shell with the long pin and finally popped into his mouth. He really enjoyed them--part of his memories of growing up in East London. Tony and I never tried them but I 'm sure we had a lollipop or an apple to eat. Then we would proceed to visit the open-air stalls and 'costermonger' barrows loaded with wonderful things and the cockney salesmen with their strange talk and begging us to buy. Daddy would get lots of big sweet-smelling oranges to put in the bottom of the sack, boxes of chocolates and Turkish delight for our mother, more fruit and a turkey.

No frozen dressed turkeys in those days! I think they had been plucked but the insides were still untouched. They hung by big yellow scaly clawlike feet with heads hanging down on long scrawny necks, bright yellow beaks, red wattles and a few stray feathers. When he got them home, he would hang the turkey by its feet over the top of the kitchen door, slam the door (securing the turkey) and then pull on the bird. It would remove its feet and pull all the tendons out of the legs too!

The shopping night was exciting for Tony and me and riding on the bus with Daddy was a treat and shopping in the noisy crowded market and hanging on to Daddy so we didn't get lost. With the quiet ride back home, I was tired but happy and wondering what Christmas day would bring. Although I can't remember any specific gifts, I know we always got something special. Uncle Georges, mother's brother, sent us a book every year; nice books, sometimes bible stories. The postman would bring a parcel from a big London shop, usually Selfridges in the West End, with a book for Tony and me. Daddy took us to London once to see Selfridges at Christmas time. It was brightly lit and had wonderful scenes in the windows. It was a marvelous, elegant store—several stories high with wide-open spacious aisles, beautifully decorated and very expensive merchandise. It was owned by an American and was a great attraction covering a whole block on Oxford Street, a fashionable street of high-class shops. It is still there!

Living in Bexleyheath we had to walk further to do the shopping but there were also people who came to the door with goods. The milkman and his horse with crates of milk bottles came around every day with butter, cream and milk. The small lorry from the baker shop brought bread and the greengrocer with his horse (pulling a cart loaded with apples, potatoes, greens, carrots, etc.) came by several times a week. Dark-skinned Spanish men from the Continent and wearing berets rode bicycles with strings of large Spanish onions on the handlebars, selling to eager housewives. A rag and bone man came down the street with his horse and cart calling out as he went, hoping that people would sell him their old clothes and furniture. A man came by on a bicycle carrying ladders on a little sidecar and offering to wash windows for a couple of shillings.

Washing day was different at our new home too. At our previous home on Sidcup Hill we had a scullery behind the kitchen where the cooking and the washing were done. In one corner of the room there was a built-in brick 'copper' for boiling the clothes and over by the window was a sink and nearby a cooking stove. Monday was always washing day and sometimes Mummy had a woman help her. The fire was lit under the copper, the laundry loaded into the copper, the slatted wooden lid put on the top and the sheets and towels boiled—the room full of steam. Some clothes were washed in the sink, scrubbed on a board with everything hung on a line in the back garden.

But on Marlborough Road there was no copper and Mummy boiled the clothes in a big pot on the cooker in the kitchen. There did not seem to be as many things to wash, the room was much smaller and for some reason the process seemed easier. Ironing day was Tuesday. She ironed on the towel-padded small wooden kitchen table with an iron that had to be heated on the cooker. Everything was ironed in those days: sheets, towels and underwear too. I don't ever remember being asked to help with the housework; Mummy kept everything neat and tidy. We had to make our own beds and Tony and I had to do the washing up (that is, wash the dishes after each evening meal) often fighting over who was going to wash and who was going to dry! There was a race to see who desperately needed to get to the bathroom first as a way out of the job. We were not allowed to go upstairs unnecessarily as Mummy believed it would cause more dust and make extra work. Things that needed to go upstairs were put on the bottom step until someone had a definite reason to go up.

Mummy was not a particularly good cook. I'm sure that she tried but not having much money, and the shortage of food in later years, made it difficult for her. We always had enough to eat. If we were ill when we were little, we got a poached egg with mashed potatoes, which has been 'comfort food' for me to this day. We liked her Shepherd's Pie and rabbit stew. I hated porridge but that didn't stop her from giving it to me and making me eat it! She always served our plates and we were not supposed to leave anything on them—"remember the starving children in Africa" was a favorite phrase. She had a very large edition (about eight inches thick) of Mrs. Beeton's Book of Household Management, first published in 1861, which had recipes and tips about housekeeping and wonderful pictures of glorious Victorian desserts and food presentations. Tony and I loved to look at it. I don't think I did any cooking until I was married; she ran the kitchen. During our summer holidays from school, she made lovely jam and we would help her shell peas and cut beans at times, usually sitting in the sun in the back garden.

Our outings with Mummy were few and far between—only to see her mother in Walthamstow, East London, or her sister, Jeanne in Streatham, Southeast London.

Renée, William, Auntie Jeanne, Joy and Tony Sidcup Hill
~ 1931

Auntie Jeanne, her husband Stephen Belloni and daughter Jasmine lived in a lovely house with Louis XVI style furniture in the drawing room; very fashionable but not practical for visiting children. They also had a fishpond in their back garden which fascinated us. Auntie Jeanne made custom hats in her home for society ladies and Uncle Steve made fur coats and capes for royalty. During the war, he was also a reserve policeman helping keep order during the devastation of air raids. Jasmine Stephanie Belloni, our cousin was born about 1933 and was a very pretty but very quiet little girl.

We loved to go their house, checking on the fishpond and the hats in the upstairs workroom and trying to make out the picture on their newest purchase, a television set! It was strange to us; we were used to listening to the wireless but to see a picture on a screen was unbelievable. In truth we couldn't see much; the screen was about six inches square though the set itself was very large, the picture was blurry. Television only made a very brief stay in England in the 1930s as more and more trouble was looming in Europe and sad days were soon to come. As children we were beginning to learn a bit more about world happenings in school and would see the newsboys' banners on the way home. Auntie Jeanne died in 1946, age 52, of throat cancer and Uncle Steve continued to live in the same house until he died at age 93.

Once in a while, Mummy would take us to the pictures. I remember seeing Freddie Bartholomew in 'Little Lord Fauntleroy' and 'David Copperfield' which I remember as very dramatic. We saw a couple of Fred Astaire films and also Sonja Henie. We watched the movie 'Gone with the Wind' with her too. As we grew older she took us to pantomimes in the London theatres.

In the late 1930s, Tony and I were busy with school and homework, Girl Guides and Scouts. For a while we went to the Baptist Church in Bexleyheath Broadway for Sunday school but England was having trouble with Germany and Mummy didn't want us so far from home. Eventually we stopped going. Neville Chamberlain went to Germany to meet with Adolf Hitler, who had invaded Austria and then Czechoslovakia. England and France wanted him to stop and Chamberlain came home telling us there would be "peace in our time." It was obviously not a sure thing as the English people started putting up blackout curtains, gas masks were issued, air raid shelters were built and preparations were made for war.

Once again our life was to change.

Chapter Three

DARTFORD COUNTY SCHOOL FOR GIRLS

Tony and I now attend different schools. War is imminent; sad circumstances break up the family. War starts and nothing is ever the same again. We march on, each to our own program and, sadly, Ma is left alone.

In 1936, when I was 11, it was time for me to take my scholarship exam, the exam that decides if you are qualified for high school or should attend a technical school. I had been going to Brampton Road Elementary School since our family had moved to Bexleyheath in 1935. I can't remember where I took the exam but I will remember forever that I did not pass it! My poor mother was heartbroken; I cannot remember my own reactions. I knew I had always expected to go high school. We were rather poor, owing to my father's health and his inability to work full-time and Dartford County School was a fee-paying school.

Dartford County School for Girls

My mother was determined; she wanted me to be allowed to take the exam again, especially as my schoolwork earned good marks and I showed good promise. I can remember her setting off with a determined air, for an appointment at the school with her hat, gloves, and purse on her arm; what transpired I never knew. I did not retake the exam although I went to the school; my mother must have agreed to do her best to pay my fees. Having gained admittance to the school, I now had to have an expensive uniform which was only obtainable from one shop in Dartford called 'Potts.' Ma was shocked at the price and was finally able to purchase the correct fabric and make my clothes herself; she was good at tailoring and was pleased with the results.

I always knew they were a bit different, but after a while I must have forgotten because I can't remember it bothering me. In winter, we wore a dark green tunic of a woolen fabric; it was a pleated sleeveless dress hanging from a square yoke with topstitching and a wide, topstitched belt. Underneath we wore a cream colored, square-necked, long sleeved blouse; I think the fabric was called 'Tobralco.' My mother had to design the pattern for this whole outfit as it was exclusive to our school; they didn't print patterns as they expected everything to be bought ready-made. This was a major project for Ma but she was clever with the needle and really did all she could to have me going to school looking like all the other girls. We wore lisle stockings, black shoes, a black velour hat with the school hatband and a dark coat and carried our gym clothes in a drawstring bag. In the summer we wore checked cotton dresses (choice of pink, green or blue and white) with white collars and cuffs and a Panama straw hat with a ribbon band of the school colors (dark green, cream and maroon) around the crown. Owing to the war and clothes rationing, my father's illness and death and my mother's expert care and alterations—that outfit lasted me the five years I went to the school!

Our school days were long, I believe from 8 a.m. to 4 p.m. And after war started, I do know that in winter we always rode home on the bus in the dark, the blackout, no streetlights, lights on cars and buses were hooded to dim them, traffic lights, too. People smoking were cautioned not to light a match in the open; even the glint of a burning cigarette could be seen at a distance. Darkness was heavy and complete for our safety. We often heard the air raid wardens shouting, "Put that light out!"

The second winter of the war we went on double daylight savings time, two hours ahead of the sun (Greenwich Mean Time) which gave us much lighter evenings and longer daylight working hours. I rode the public trolley bus from 'The Crook Log,' a pub on the border of Bexleyheath and Welling to West Hill Schools in Dartford. Arriving at Bexleyheath Clock Tower, a transfer stop on the way home, was always interesting because the newspaper boys were there with their posters crying out the latest news of the Royal Family, the Silver Jubilee of George V (1935) and his illness and death (1936), the abdication of Edward VIII (1936), and the coronation of George VI (1937). Neville Chamberlain's return from Munich in 1938 and the invasion of Poland in 1939 were tense. The days of Dunkirk in 1940 were dark and depressing but all were interesting and exciting times, which we learned about through the newspaper boy's shouted enthusiasm.

I was going to an all-girls school five miles from home; the boy's school was close to ours and they rode the same buses but not at the same time! The starting bell rang earlier at the Grammar School for Boys so they rode earlier buses. It was the same at the end of day, done so that we would not associate with the boys and get into mischief on the public buses. Many of the men who worked on the buses (drivers and conductors) were called into the army and we had women bus conductors during the war, some of them stricter than the men had been with us. The boy's school playing field was over the fence from ours but heaven help us if we were caught looking at the boys over the fence; we could be in real trouble with the headmistress.

Our Headmistress, Miss E. M. Fryer, was a formidable woman to an 11-year old girl. She was tall and dressed mostly in long gray skirts and jumpers (sweaters), old-fashioned orthopedic shoes and her grey hair drawn back tightly in a bun. Eventually, through my years there, I grew to realize that she was very fair and quite kind and I think enjoyed all the girls in her care. She had a difficult job, for during her time there as headmistress, England went to war with Germany.

On March 31, 2003, this Dartford County School memoir chapter and the following one (September 3, 1939: WWII Declared) were sent as historical records to the Dartford County School for Girls, as they prepared for their 100th anniversary celebration to occur in 2004.

Chapter Four

SEPTEMBER 3, 1939: WWII DECLARED

S chool in wartime was scary. We had to carry our gas masks to school each day and always have them near. At first they came in cardboard boxes with a string handle but the boxes deteriorated fast. Also, the government issued extensions to the gas mask itself so we were provided a metal canister to carry them in. It was quite fashionable to knit or sew an outer cover for it to match your coat. We would have 15-minute sessions of wearing the masks in class. They smelled awful and steamed up so one could not see. But the Germans never used gas in World War II so we were lucky; they were never used as designed.

School lessons were conducted in trenches that had been dug in the school playgrounds even before the war started. The government wanted to be ready for whatever might happen. They called them trenches but were a form of air raid shelters, concrete tunnels zigzagging through the earth. Earth piled on top made it look as if a giant mole had burrowed under the sports field. We went down steps into this large concrete tunnel with wooden slatted floors and wooden benches down the sides. The walls were always running with water that seeped through the concrete and pooled under the slatted floors. To this day I have nightmares about seeping concrete walls and I have always hated basements and similar buildings. They were dimly lit and it was not possible to see very far because the trenches angled every few feet. The idea being that if a bomb dropped near the entrance the blast would only go as far as the first angle; it couldn't go around the bend. We never got to check this theory because the bombs that did drop on the school grounds did not harm the air-raid shelters. Years later, I learned they had been covered over immediately after the war and were only rediscovered in the 1980s when digging foundations for new buildings.

We gathered twice a week in the shelters to receive our homework and to get a little instruction from our teachers. There was a government regulation forbidding large gatherings in case of air raids. So the classes were divided and each group stayed two or three hours each time; we did the large part of our schoolwork alone at home. It was amazing that so many of us were able to pass our school leaving certificate examination; we were practically self-educated.

School as a daily routine was out of the question for at least a year and a half, definitely after the fall of Paris and the Dunkirk evacuation in 1940, all during the Battle of Britain and the Blitz. Books were in short supply in those days and paper very scarce. We had to write small and on every inch, no margins or headings, and sometimes we even wrote on rough brown paper. The newspapers were very small, only one double sheet, and nothing was wrapped up or put in a bag in the shops. Yet maybe we were the lucky ones.

The government evacuated many, many children to the safer areas of the country and some even as far as Canada. That proved to be a tragedy, for the first ship with evacuees going to Canada was torpedoed in the Atlantic. Many of those who left never saw their parents again or were often placed in homes they hated with people who didn't want them. They were treated badly; they were unhappy and so were their hosts. I think people who lived out in the countryside were obligated to take evacuees if they had a spare room. We were eligible but our parents, especially, said a definite "NO." It had turned out to be a very sad situation and our mother was right in keeping us with her. Queen Elizabeth had the same feelings. She was reported to have said, "I am staying here beside my husband (King George VI) who cannot leave the Londoners, I cannot leave the King, and my children will stay here with me," or words to that effect. The children, Princesses Elizabeth and Margaret Rose, spent most of the war at Windsor Castle, west of London. The King and Queen frequently visited heavily-bombed areas and homeless bombed-out people, speaking kindly with them; they were very much loved during the war. Buckingham Palace, the home of the King and Queen was bombed more than once.

It was during this time, after the fall of France, that we were preparing more and more each day for the invasion. Church bells were silenced as they were to be used as a warning that the enemy had arrived on our shores; it was a miracle that the Germans never came.

Air raids were a constant problem, especially during the Battle of Britain 1940-1941 and the Blitz that followed, when we hardly ever got a full night's sleep. At first we were offered an Anderson shelter to bury in our back garden. It was to be buried halfway and then covered with several inches of dirt and would hold six people on wooden slatted bunks. Its biggest problem was the lack of drainage. England has a lot of rain and it would collect in the shelter; also with a bomb exploding nearby, one ran the risk of being buried alive. My mother preferred that our family slept in the cupboard under the stairs and later (when the government designed an alternative) we were issued a Morrison shelter, a heavy steel table installed indoors. We put it up in the dining room and we all slept under that on mattresses.

Using the Morrison shelter as a table.

We also kept a small water supply in our bath, in case the water mains should be broken during the raids, or we needed it to put out fires. When we took a bath, we were only allowed four inches of water. Coal was rationed and although we had a fireplace in every room in the house, we only used the one in the dining room. It was a scary and very noisy time.

During the Blitz, which followed the Battle of Britain, there was a constant drone of planes, the firing of anti-aircraft guns mounted in the nearby park, the swooshing and clatters of bombs and the rattle of shrapnel—all made for restless and sleepless nights. The sky was full of barrage balloons that sometimes caught fire and had to be shot down. People ventured out of their shelters when the 'all clear" sounded—often to find their home a pile of rubble, flooded from a broken water main or bombed gas mains spouting 40-foot flames after being hit. One never quite knew what to expect.

As a group war effort, we students raised pigs! Two pigs were given us; we were to supply scraps to feed them. An assembly was held and Miss Fryer talked to us about naming the pigs. Needless to say, they were girl pigs; we were all allowed to submit ideas if we wished but were not allowed to use the name of any girl in the school. They were named Arabella and Priscilla; whenever I hear those names I think of the school's war effort! We spent lots of time leaning over the wall of the pen watching them, a bit smelly, but interesting. When they were almost full-grown, one of 'Hitler's messengers' (a term for bomber pilots) dropped a bomb beside their pen. The brick-built pen was shattered but strangely the pigs were not hurt—just loose! I think they must have run off a lot of fat before they were finally caught a couple of days later. The pigs were butchered, the pen was rebuilt and although we had a couple more pigs, the excitement was gone. In fact, I don't think the second two were ever named!

During the war "Waste not, Want not" was a common motto. Chained to the lampposts on the city streets (which were not lighted for more than five years during the blackout) were dustbins, garbage cans, supplied by the government. Into these, everybody was to put all leftover food scraps to feed the country's pigs. A lorry (truck) came around regularly to empty the bins and take the food to the farmers. I think the fattened pigs must have gone to the troops. I do know that meat was almost nonexistent in our shops and severely rationed for many years;

I believe until 1953. Other mottos I remember were "Is your journey really necessary?" "Even walls have ears" or "Careless talk costs lives," encouraging us not to talk about the war, the location of our soldiers or of war materiel production and "Coughs and sneezes spread diseases" encouraging us to cover our sneezes. Many people had coughs and skin diseases during the war from overcrowding. Many hundreds of people slept night after night in the London Underground on the platforms and on the tracks, after the last train of the night had finished its run. People whose homes were destroyed by bombs had to crowd in with friends and relatives. The constant crowding allowed diseases to spread rapidly, shelters were often packed full of frightened people.

As the war progressed, shortages became greater. Lots of planes had been destroyed; metal was needed to build new ones and the government put out an appeal to housewives to sacrifice some of their saucepans. Thousands of saucepans were gathered but there was never any information given out to inform the people if they had been used; many people believed that they were still piled around and never used as planned.

The schoolgirls were divided into six houses, which were named after the Houses of British Royalty: Plantagenet, York, Lancaster, Tudor, Stuart, and Windsor. This was for competition and sports, though sports were not too important during the bad years of the war. I was in Plantagenet. We rarely excelled in anything and were nearly always the lowest on the totem pole! It seemed York and Lancaster houses won most of the honors. This I believe to be true, though more than 70 years may have dimmed my memory. I think Miss Carter was our English teacher and a Miss Lewin nicknamed 'Dobbin' taught geography but I remember no others. I can recall some assemblies, classes in the tower and the names of several of the girls. My classes were named 2G1, meaning second year, German instruction, class one (3G1, 4G1, etc.)

In the summer of 1941, it was time to take my school leaving examination. I had studied English, math (arithmetic, algebra, and geometry), history, geography, science (biology, chemistry and general science), French for five years and German (even though they were our enemy) for four. There had been some art classes, sewing, physical education, most of which I don't remember. We had music and sang the scales up to the words: "The poplar leaves are growing fast" and down—"The poplar leaves are falling fast," while glancing out of the window to see the poplar trees along the edge of the school grounds. We played tennis, rounders (a type of softball) and hockey in the winter. I was not comfortable with sports or physical education and would like to have got out of it!

Before the war, the class went to Dartford Public Swimming Pool for lessons; the worst class I had to take. I absolutely froze, turned blue, and couldn't breathe. I would have probably drowned if they had insisted I continue. But it wasn't all peaches and cream to be excused from the lesson; I had to stay in the classroom and do homework instead! We had no extracurricular activities like clubs, dances or proms. I do remember going to the Royal Albert Hall in Kensington, West London to watch a group from Spain sing and dance but that was just before the war. It was interesting because they wore Spanish dress, which I had never seen except in pictures. And every time the audience applauded, they started to dance again; they had to be coaxed off the stage.

Now, back to that dreaded school leaving examination. I could do reasonably well with term work but always froze in exams. I don't remember the actual tests, but "Oh," the excitement I felt when, during the summer holidays, the postman brought the results. I had passed! Not only passed but gained matriculation exemption as well, a qualification for entrance to the University of London. I still have the certificate with Miss Fryer's letter. I was eager to become a research chemist and Burroughs Welcome had a laboratory in Dartford (close to the school); I knew what I was going to do as a career! But our lives changed and it was never to be. To this day, I think about what might have been.

My father was ill; he had been wounded and gassed in what was then known as 'The Great War.' He had been in ill health ever since. And now with another war—going to his job as a dairy inspector each day at 4 a.m., riding his bike through the blackout, and having to stay awake most nights because of air raids—he was worried about falling incendiary bombs. These bombs would come down in large numbers, many of them explosive when water was used to try to extinguish them and only sandbags would smother them.

Daddy was truly failing. His father, who had been moved out of his home by the government because of the frequent air raids on the coast and the airport adjoining his property, died in another son's home North of London in January 1941. Daddy had to take care of his affairs. Then he crashed into a wall while riding his bicycle in the blackout and destroyed all his front teeth. He was becoming weaker and although I knew these things, it wasn't until later I realized how serious the situation was.

Miss Fryer was convinced that I would be employed as a laboratory apprentice at Burroughs Welcome but it would take time. So, I was invited to join the sixth form, a group of girls who were going on to university in due course.

In England, at that time, a student took the school leaving exam at 16 but could not enter university until 18; hence the sixth form for extra and specialized studies. I was to concentrate on math and science which worked fine for a couple of months.

Then one day in November 1941, my father surprised me with a trip to London on the train, to an income tax office in Moorgate for a job interview. I got the job to start the following week, earning 25 shillings a week (just over five dollars). I was so upset! This was not the career I dreamed of for so long; I couldn't believe this was happening. I went to school the next day and told Miss Fryer. She said she had got me the job in the lab and to tell my parents. Hope soared again but my parents said, "No!" My father, a very kind and gentle man talked to me and said that he was too ill to work and they needed me to work and help support the family (I had two younger brothers) with my pay. He promised me that when he got better I could try again for lab work, but at that time the government job was more secure and would keep me from being called up for the army (women were conscripted in those days).

One week later, my father died. Tony and I were not allowed to go to his funeral. On that day I went to the office and was so distraught that an older coworker took me out of the office for the day, bought me a brandy and lunch and comforted me until it was time to take the train home. I'll never forget her name, Nadia Penty, or the date, Monday, December 8, 1941. Is it any wonder that it was a long time before the events of the previous day (Pearl Harbor) registered with me?

I worked unenthusiastically for the government, searching old records to trace people who had not paid their income tax. Most of the time it was because they had been killed in the war as servicemen overseas or civilians in air raids, not a satisfying result for the government or me. I stayed with them until after I was married in 1945, working in several different offices scattered around London.

Joy at 16 after passing her exams ~ 1941

In 1996, I was visiting in England and my 91 year-old Aunt Bessie died. On the way to her funeral my brother, Geoffrey, and I drove past Dartford County (now Grammar) School for Girls in Shepherds Lane. He stopped the car in front of the school. It was very impressive; built to resemble a castle with its crenellated tower and grey stone walls even though it had only been built in 1904. Since my time there, lots of classrooms had been added on the sides and back, to the point where there are no longer any tennis courts or sports playing fields visible from the road. We had time and my brother suggested I go in. I'm so glad I did! They gave me a great welcome. Two students took me to the old science lab, pointed out the 'antique' student lockers in the halls (which hadn't changed since my time except to become more dilapidated) and extended an invitation to come back again. They still have the records of every girl that went there and I was thrilled to receive mine.

In the year 2004, I attended the 100th anniversary of the school and, although I recognized no one from my classes, I had a delightful afternoon with a girl who had been e-mailing me the details of the event. We had lunch together, watched a short skit about present day life in the school and learned of some of new changes in effect today. It became a day to remember!

Chapter Five

ENGLAND AT WAR

1 941 had not been a good year for our family. The bombers came every night, loaded with incendiaries and high explosive bombs. My grandfather had died in January after catching pneumonia. He was on a journey to his home adjoining Manston Airport on the coast of Kent from which he had been evacuated. He had wanted to mend a fence that had blown down in an air raid; it was a sad ending to his life.

Neighbors had been killed and bombs had destroyed houses across the street and around the corner from us. My father had a bicycle accident in the blackout; my mother was hysterical because he was so ill. We never seemed to get a good night's sleep and our house had been damaged, walls cracked and roof blown off and I was asked to quit school and go to work.

Rationing had also become more severe. Long gone were the days when the shopkeeper cut your piece of cheese off a large wheel with a wire, or patted your cube of butter with two wooden paddles from a large block. Tea, jam, biscuits and other items the English enjoyed were put on a points system that added pages to our ration books. With the points system, you could have an either or choice; like either tea or jam. Sweets and cakes were rationed too. Whale meat was now on the market and dried milk and powdered eggs or eggs preserved in isinglass were available. None of these items were popular with the average Englishman; we ate a lot of things that seemed undesirable and inedible. Enemy activity in the North Sea made fishing dangerous and even though fish was not rationed, the fish counters were often empty. I could remember the pre-war fish shops with fish of every kind laid on marble slabs: herring, mackerel, haddock, cod, plaice, salmon and sole. There were eels swimming in tubs, tiny pink shrimp and smoked kippers!

Sadly, 1942 did not start well either. Every winter during the war seemed to bring worse weather than we had seen in years with very sharp and cold east winds and many weeks of snow that was slow in melting. Often the London fog was so thick it was hard to find the corners of the pavement. Bus conductors were leading the buses at about five miles an hour, guiding them with a flare or a torch highlighting the curb, trying to make it through the dense fog. Many times they just shut down and went back to the garage. The Bexleyheath bus garage received a direct hit in an air raid, destroying many trolley buses and the building.

Daddy had died. Now our Beaver relations decided that our mother could not look after, nor afford to maintain three children. She was just devastated at the loss of our father and the damaged state of our home. To help her, they proposed to have Tony leave school, The Dartford Grammar School where he was doing so well. He was only 13 and had at least three more years to go. Their idea was for him to live in Stanmore, Middlesex (North of London) with Uncle Henry Beaver and Cousin Alan, who was a couple of years younger than Tony. They proposed he go to work with Henry at the G.P.O (General Post Office) as a telegraph boy. In those years a telegraph or telegram boy was a regular Post Office employee, who rode a bicycle with a basket on the front handlebars to hold telegrams and deliver them all over town.

Telegrams were important in those days; they carried good and bad news. They were messages to say a serviceman was coming home on leave, leaving for duty elsewhere, or missing in or killed in action. Families were reporting bomb damaged homes or a relative's death in an air raid; these young boys delivered those messages. The idea was that Tony might establish a future in the Post Office. I guess Ma said "Yes;" I can't imagine why. Here we had lost Daddy and now we were losing Tony too. I was devastated and Ma was so hysterical that I hardly wanted to go home from work. She hung on to Geoffrey's hand and would not let him out of her sight.

I realize now I was no help to her. I was working in London, fascinated with the City and the West End. I loved all the historic places, the cinemas and the theatres; it was so easy to take a later train home. I was a loner and I would sit in the churches or walk in the parks alone. St. Paul's

Cathedral was one of my favorite places and just a short walk from my office. I always took sandwiches from home for lunch and I would eat them while working and so had my whole lunch hour to walk around the City. I did not have much money as most of my paycheck went to my mother. I was given enough to buy my train ticket so that I could get to work each day. I went early, as the tickets were cheaper before 7:30 a.m. I was allowed very little spending money but I was happy walking and exploring.

Much of the City of London and many buildings in the West End had been destroyed in the air raids. There were many open areas, some were still rubble covered, and we were still under attack from the air. Months went by and after the summer of 1944, air raids were no longer Junkers 88 and Messerschmitt planes. The enemy was sending pilotless V1's and V2's, totally different to plane engines roaring overhead. V2's made no sound until they reached the ground and exploded, devastating large areas and killing many who had no warning of danger. They were Germany's Vengeance weapons fired across the English Channel from the now Nazi-occupied France. Once again, we seemed to learn how to live with whatever the enemy was sending our way.

Auntie Winnie, Daddy's youngest sister, lived with us during the months after he died. In the summer of 1942, she planned a holiday in Minehead, Somerset in the West of England and wanted me to travel with her. I think everyone was concerned about me as I missed Daddy and Tony so much. Ma agreed and we traveled by coach with a group.

On the second day, we were walking on the moors and for some unknown reason I started running down a steep slope and couldn't stop. A man from the group reached out to stop me and I slid and went down on one knee in the gravelly ground. I ended up in the hospital and then spent the rest of the trip in a wheelchair! What a sad ending for Auntie Winnie's holiday. I remember being in a wheelchair for several weeks after I returned home; I still have a scarred knee to this day.

I think that made our mother see things differently as Tony was brought home and transferred to the Bexleyheath Post Office to continue his job. He was not allowed to return to school. I, too, was transferred from my London office to a local one in Bexleyheath and continued my search for non-paying income tax persons. So Ma got back control of her children and Auntie Winnie moved out. My leg gave me lots of trouble and I remember being in a wheelchair again later. Tony would take me for walks in Danson Park; it had a steep hill which made me nervous but excited with his erratic piloting of the chair.

That Christmas, Ma too worked for the Post Office delivering mail for the holiday season and with the holiday we were a family back together.

Despite the air raids, evenings at home became fun. Tony's friends, Derek and Barney (Peter), would come over every night and play records for hours and as loud as possible; they had a large collection of jazz and popular songs. Anything they did not like, they would throw out the window they always kept open. Years later, I learned that Geoffrey would gather them up and still has them to this day! They would ride their bikes during air raids, checking new bombsites and the damage. Boys were more adventuresome during and after air raids and they were eager to gather bits of shrapnel or pieces of downed planes. Girls were kept more at home, to be protected, though they loved it if anyone found a discarded parachute for them—they were wonderful fabric.

Ma would listen to the BBC news and all Winston Churchill speeches, which were always encouraging. Defeat was never in his plans; he was positive that England would win the war. Late at night 'Lord HawHaw,' a pro-Nazi Englishman was broadcasting from Germany; Ma found him serious and the boys thought he was hilarious. Our evenings were fun but we still slept on the dining room floor, crawling on our hands and knees to get under the Morrison shelter, hoping it would protect us one more night.

In June of 1944, government workers were offered an opportunity to help the Land Army girls with their farm work. We would get a week off work, a train ticket, sleep in tents and harvest potatoes in Winchester—a town in Southern England. It sounded like a good chance to get away from the office. So, with Ma's permission, I signed up. The first couple of days we worked as planned and went sightseeing in Winchester, touring the Cathedral started by William the Conqueror in the 11th century and visiting the Round Table of King Arthur and his knights.

Ma at Marlborough Road during WWII

On the next evening, we heard the sound of heavy traffic and several of us walked to the main road to see what was happening. There were long, long convoys of tanks, trucks, guns, soldiers marching on foot, military officers riding in cars and jeeps with planes flying overhead. The Allies were about to invade Normandy, the night before D-Day— June 6, 1944. We watched for hours. So many men going off to war but a rough sea to cross first, yet they were in high spirits. We did not want to leave and go back to our tents. I don't think we even worked the next day with the sky full of barrage balloons and the never ending convoy—it was more exciting to stand and watch history being made.

Later that year, I started going to the local dance hall in Welling, the Embassy Ballroom. Though I didn't dance very well (little sense of rhythm) I enjoyed the people whom I met there. There were always a lot of servicemen, mostly Americans. I did meet some Australian and New Zealand pilots, stationed at nearby airports (Croyden or Biggin Hill). However, they never stayed around very long; maybe they were transferred or, sadly, killed in action. The pilots were young, exciting and glamorous, risking their lives every time they flew.

I was just 19 when I met Carl Beebe there in September 1944. He was serving with the U. S. Army Signal Corps and had been in England for several months. He was stationed in an old castle called 'Hall Place' in Old Bexley, about three miles from my home and the village where Daddy's dairy job had been. Carl didn't dance; he told me his parents were quite religious and did not believe in dancing or drinking. They didn't even have instrumental music in their church. He had come to the dance hall with his army buddies; some of them I knew because they had been coming there often. This was the first time I had seen Carl (it may have been his first visit) and we were introduced, standing right in the front entrance. He told me then he didn't dance so I wandered off and probably danced with someone who did. Anyway, he kept coming whenever he had a night off and, finally, talked me into going out with him.

Chapter Six

THOUGHTS ON MY LIFE, AS CARL BECOMES MY FRIEND

T he English had been at war for a long time— since September 3, 1939. I remember many events leading up to that day. Britain's Prime Minister Neville Chamberlain went to Germany when Hitler invaded Czechoslovakia in 1938, and came back telling us "there will be peace in our time." Many people found that hard to believe; there were 'brown shirts,' Nazi followers in our country and had been for quite a while. People were digging air raid shelters in their back yards and making heavy black curtains for their windows to comply with the new 'blackout' rules. County governments were building cement air raid shelters near parks and shopping centers and the government issued us with gas masks.

September 1, 1939 Hitler invaded Poland and the British Government gave him until Sunday the third to retreat. It is history: England declared war Sunday morning. September 3. The King, George VI, and the Prime Minister, Neville Chamberlain, spoke to the nation on the radio. The whole country listened; we were at war!! And within minutes the air raid sirens sounded!! Luckily, it was only a false alarm.

My brother, Tony, and I had been sent to our bedrooms because we were too young to understand, according to our mother. We sat at the top of the stairs and could hear the voices on the radio and our mother crying, Daddy trying to comfort her. Many persons of her age were terrified at the idea of another war. They had lived through a very nasty one from 1914-1918 and just over 20 years had not been long enough to erase the horrors they had suffered. Things were quiet for a long time with only an occasional air raid; but after the Germans broke through Belgium and into France in 1940, things were never quiet again for a long time. A large pall of depression hung over England in June of 1940, as Germans pushed our soldiers into the sea at Dunkirk. We could hear the noise of the gunfire coming from the French coast; thousands of heroic people manned boats to bring home the men across the treacherous English Channel. It is only 22 miles from Calais to Dover but a very rough sea. Everyone knew what was going on; the fear that the Germans were now so close was uppermost in our minds.

Gun emplacements and concrete blockhouses were built along the main roads. Church bells were silent, only to be rung to warn us of the enemy's arrival on our shores. People stayed off the streets. At the end of August 1940, the planes fighting in the skies and bombing raids started in earnest. The Home Guard watched from rooftops; we all prepared and waited for the invasion. Eventually the enemy changed their plans and never invaded us by land, still bombing us night and day by air!

By the time I met Carl we had suffered air raids, bombings by V1 and V2 rockets, and rationing of food, clothes, household goods, furniture. Many things had been totally unobtainable for years. We also had a large 'invasion' of foreign soldiers, sailors and airmen. When the war first started there were many restrictions: theatres and cinemas closed, people were not allowed to congregate in large groups and school limited to two days a week in small groups with class attendance in air raid shelters and most lessons to study at home.

Nights were spent sleeping in the cupboard under the stairs until the government issued us a 'Morrison Shelter.' Night after night the air raid sirens would sound. The Germans would fly over in waves headed for London and the docks, only a few miles west of our town as the crow, or an airplane, would fly. Bombing raids were not always the same. There were heavy bombs that destroyed whole streets of houses, or incendiary raids where hundreds of small fire-bombs were dropped. Fires erupted everywhere on contact: on roofs, porches, by gates and sheds. If they were near something combustible, the fires raged in a hurry.

For three days and nights in the late 1940s, the German planes bombed the London docks and the City of London business district. Fires burned for days after and were visible for miles—St. Paul's Cathedral stood alone amidst piles of rubble and burning ashes.

Another type of weapon was the land mine. This bomb drifted down on a parachute and made a broad but shallow crater, shattering everything within a large radius. It would take out whole streets of houses, shatter glass and strip the tiles off roofs for miles around. Several times during the raids all the tiles were blown off the roof of our house, leaving us wide open to the weather until someone could cover it up. Our windows were broken and glass was not replaced until after the war. The window frames were covered with a heavy linen-like fabric that fluttered constantly in the wind with noisy flapping sounds; they often blew out again with the blast from another bomb.

Glass was extremely dangerous. Bomb blasts would shatter the windows with such a force that the glass would bury itself in splinters deeply in the opposite wall, penetrate books on a bookshelf or tear into a person's flesh. Many people had blue scars on their faces from having been in line of shattering glass. The safest place, if you were in a room with large glass windows, would be to lie on the floor directly beneath the windows. The glass would always shoot forward across the room, rarely downward. Despite much damage we were never forced to leave our home, though we were often quite cold and very uncomfortable. There were phosphorous bombs that burned in the bottom of craters for weeks and would explode when doused with water.

Later in the war, we were attacked with VI and V2 rockets fired toward London from the coast of France. One of the worst incidents was in Crayford, a town about three miles away, where the children were lined up outside the school ready to get on the buses to be evacuated to a safer area. They received a direct hit from a V2 rocket and about 100 children were killed. The American soldiers stationed at Hall Place,

including Carl, were involved in taking care of this disaster; something
he remembered forever!

The V2 was the most devastating bomb of WWII, they made no
sound until they hit the ground; you had no chance to run from them!
Of course London was not the only town bombed; towns and villages
all over England and Scotland were attacked. I lived in Kent (Southeast
of London) which is in a direct line between London and the coasts of
England and France, an area known at the time as 'bomb alley.'

When planes coming from Germany or France met with anti-aircraft
fire from our defending guns or battled with Spitfire or Hurricane fighters, they were often shot down or damaged and would jettison their
bombs. If they made it all the way to their target, they often seemed to
save one last bomb for us on their way home! The sky was full of barrage
balloons, huge silver blimps on guy wires, a defense against attacking
aircraft; sometimes they caught fire producing a great blazing ball in the
sky and sometimes they broke loose and drifted. On D-Day 1944 there
were hundreds of them in the sky.

We had anti-aircraft guns mounted in the local park and on railway
flat cars that ran up and down railway lines near our house, probably manned by the A.T.S. (Auxiliary Territorial Service), the women's
branch of the army. These were rocket guns that were in tiers firing
one tier after another right over our house; the noise was deafening
and terrifying. Planes that were hit screamed as they came down, so did
'Molotov Cocktails,' a screaming fire bomb filled with shrapnel. Junkers
88 used to scream as they dive-bombed or machine-gunned places like
railway stations and high streets. There were dogfights in the sky between
our fighters and the German planes.

My brother, Tony, and I stood in a field one Saturday afternoon when
we were sent shopping and watched a German fighter come down in
flames; the pilot dangling on a parachute drifting down near it. We
got pretty good with aircraft recognition, not only by sight but also by
sound. Our family knew sailors who had gruesome stories to tell about
life at sea and the danger of U-Boats; men who lived on our street went to
war and never came back. One little four-year-old boy on our street went
mad with fear during the air raids and would not get out from under the
table; finally, he died. The boy next door was discharged from the service

because he went out of his mind in the Navy. There were horror stories and sad situations everywhere.

On December 1, 1941, my father died; an indirect result of having been gassed in the 'Great War' (1914-1918) as it was then known. Even though people realized their lives were in danger all the time, they still got on with their jobs, rode trains and buses in air-raids, tried to live a normal life and were determined that England was going to win the war. During the Battle of Britain and the Blitz we were alone; we were the only nation fighting to save the world from the Nazis. Although we waited a long, long time for outside help, we were determined to hang on until help arrived. Winston Churchill's speeches were powerful encouragement; he knew victory would be ours.

By 1942, people were getting used to the way things were going. Shortages were serious and there was no end in sight. I think people started to think that if this was the way life would be, we had better start relaxing and enjoy things while we still could. People queued up for hours to go to the pictures; cinemas were booming, theatres ran matinees and evening performances, and famous stars could be seen for small prices. London was jammed and there was a tremendous aura of excitement in all we did. Band concerts in the parks, off-the-ration foods in restaurants (you had to queue up for hours to get in), tea dances in big hotels and dancing in the Covent Garden Opera House with a big band at each end of the ballroom.

And men! London was full of soldiers, sailors and airmen from Australia, New Zealand, Poland, France and America. It was like an invasion; every man was in uniform and from another country, and our Englishmen were fighting on the seas and in North Africa—rarely getting home. They were not too happy to see the English girls going out with foreigners; in fact, there were many serious fights in pubs and streets because the English men wanted to protect their sisters and the 'girl next door.'

As I have mentioned before, at this time I was working in the big City, very near the Tower of London. Sometimes I would take my sandwich and sit in the gardens overlooking the Tower, or walk through the city streets to St. Paul's Cathedral to spend a few quiet minutes in there. I don't believe that any churches were ever locked during the war; any time day or night you could go in and sit and absorb the peace of hundreds of years. Later, I transferred to another office and Westminster Abbey was my haven.

London has always been for me a very special place. Even after being away for 20 years, I find the same charm present upon each and every return, like going 'home.' The history, the green of the parks in the centre of a very large city, the calm of the churches and the excitement of a tour given by a Beefeater in the Tower of London are all things I very much enjoy and feel connected to. Turning a corner and seeing St. Paul's Cathedral, crossing Westminster Bridge walking toward the Houses of Parliament, the long walk down the Mall to Buckingham Palace, feeding the ducks in St. James Park—these are my first memories of London.

Mummy would only travel if it was to visit a family member and even then she often became too tired. But my father first took Tony and me there when I was six or seven years old; I still have the pictures taken of us sitting by the stone lions in Trafalgar Square. All those places are still standing today, just as I remembered them. Although London was badly bombed, most of her historic places survived.

This was my life when I met Carl and though he didn't dance, he did enjoy walking and we found many things we were happy to do together. English people walk a lot; they think nothing of walking for several miles just for something to do. We had a very large park near my home, Danson Park. It had been beautiful before the war, but now there were guns mounted there. The lake had been drained so that the reflection of the water did not guide the bombers and the public swimming pool was no longer filled or used. The English rose gardens had been neglected and no one lived anymore in the Danson Mansion House. Originally, a house had been built there about 1200 A.D and had been replaced with an elegant 18th century building, now falling into disrepair.

Carl and I spent many happy hours there just walking. I also would walk through the High street and over the hills with him back to his billet in Hall Place then catch the bus back home. Hall Place was another Manor House, dating back to 1540 A.D., which had been occupied by the U. S. Army Signal Corps during the latter part of 1943. It was known to be beautiful inside, although Carl reported that all the walls and stair well had been covered with plywood to protect them from the boots and hands of the many soldiers who worked there, intercepting and decoding messages from the Luftwaffe, the enemy Air Force.

We would go to the pictures or stop at a pub. Pubs were fun in those days and young people could legally drink at 16. They had gardens for families to enjoy; people played darts or sang and the piano was often played. There were those who had a few words to say about the Germans and the latest air raids. There was a lot of camaraderie in those days. We could get beer but wine and (scotch) whiskey was very scarce. Some publicans saved all they had for the 'Yanks' who were willing to pay more than the average Englishman.

Carl worked a different shift each week and when he could, he would take the train into London (a half-hour from my home) to the centre of the city and meet me for lunch or after I finished work and I would show him the places I loved. I can't remember when I first brought him to meet my mother; did I take him to the house or did we all meet in London and go to the theatre? I can't remember! I do recollect that we went to the theatre one very cold evening and I slipped and fell on the ice on the station hill. Carl and Ma were very concerned as it took me a while to come around.

Tony was home that Christmas of 1944 and Carl took us (Tony, Geoffrey and me) to an area where the houses had all been bombed and the trees and undergrowth had taken over; he cut a Christmas tree for us. I had never heard of cutting your own tree before; maybe because I had never lived in the countryside, only in town. Somehow Carl made us lights for it and we were all thrilled. He was always very handy around our house; repairing and building things and taught my brothers how to work with wood etc., ideas they have used all their lives.

Food was more plentiful in the American Army than it was for the British. Carl encouraged my mother's love for him by bringing home whatever he could scrounge from the cook. We were very doubtful about a jar of peanut butter he brought; we had never seen or heard of such a thing but it was a success. To this day, I never eat peanut butter without thinking of that incident! We took 'Ma' and Geoffrey to a pantomime in London right after Christmas 1944 and by then, we were already thinking that we would like to get married.

The war had been going on for over five years; there seemed to be no real sign that it would ever be over. Men were being killed by the thousands in Belgium and troops were struggling to try to cross the Rhine. Germany still showed great strength, even though things had gone badly in Russia and the V1 and V2 rockets were still coming our way.

Carl said he wanted to take me to America because he could make a better living there; I was very hesitant. I knew I didn't want to go to America and besides there was a war on! Who knew what might happen? My mother did not want me to go away; I don't suppose she really wanted me to get married but she helped us plan. She really liked Carl.

Carl and Joy, leaving the Church followed by Ma

She used to make apple dumplings especially for him and he never forgot them. She made dresses for my bridesmaids. In England, the bridesmaids are often little girls; mine were Betty Croucher (a four-year-old neighbor girl), Margaret Mercer (a ten-year-old daughter of one of my co-workers) and her cousin Barbara, who was 13.

Tony and Ma made it so that I had a beautiful wedding. As jewelry was almost impossible to buy, Ma sold her diamond engagement ring to Carl and used the money to pay for our wedding.

We were married in a church in the corner of our favorite Danson Park. It snowed as we went into the church and Tony's shoulders were white with snow. When we came out of the church, the sun was shining and several of the 'Yanks' took pictures. Geoffrey's memories of the day were precious. He was wearing his first pair of full-length trousers, having almost reached the age of 11. He had new shoes and was fascinated by the melting snow dripping into buckets placed under the bomb-damaged church roof.

Tony had bought me a wedding gown from somewhere, black market maybe! He also talked his friend's mother into making me a wedding cake.

Carl and Joy's War Time Wedding Cake ~
April 28, 1945

Where did the ingredients come from in April 1945 after six years of war?

"Don't ask," said Tony.

It was wonderful; we had the reception at our house on Marlborough Road in Bexley Heath, where I had lived since I was ten. Aunts, uncles and cousins came; it was one of the few times in my life I had ever ridden in a car.

Chapter Seven

THOUGHTS ABOUT LEAVING MY COUNTRY

When war started, travel was difficult for the average person; trains and buses were crowded with soldiers and sailors traveling to their camps or on leave. More and more servicemen came from other countries to join the war effort: Europe, Free French, Belgians and Polish. Men came from the British Empire and, after Pearl Harbor, from America and the population of London increased to 11 million.

It was only because I fell in love and married an American in 1945 that I started to travel in a big way. When I was planning my wedding I didn't realize I was sealing my fate and would have to go to America. I was not excited about that and neither was my Mother.

I really knew very little about America; in school we had learned about the 13 colonies. We knew many people emigrated there because of religious persecution, that the colonists fought the English in the Revolutionary War that started over the tea tax and that they threw English tea into Boston Harbor and then, won the war! That was the end of American history in our schoolbooks. Strange, it was as though England no longer recognized America and United States history no longer mattered. America had come into the 1914-1918 war in the last few months to help in France, after the French and the British had spent almost four years in devastating trench warfare. Americans then returned to their own country within a short time of the victory. They were involved in the peace Treaty of Versailles which was not completed for many months.

The war in 1945 had lasted so long that it was hard to imagine it ending. I was having a fabulous time in London with my new boyfriend, Carl, and didn't want that to end. It was in London that I learned of all the wonderful places a big city holds. I continued to spend my lunch hours in the City with Christopher Wren's beautiful churches or the Tower of London, exploration of historic sites and skirting bombedout areas to get to the places I wanted to see. After work there were great theatres with famous stars playing every night to enjoy. I loved 'City Life!' It was while walking in London one evening with Carl that we saw on a reader board that President Franklin D. Roosevelt had died; somehow it heralded the fact that things might change.

But the war did end. Almost six years after it had started, Adolf Hitler, Germany's dictator, took his own life the April weekend we were married; within days the war was over. In July, Carl was sent to Germany where he continued to serve in the 6811th Signal Corps with his work of copying and deciphering code. America was still at war in the Pacific and he was kept busy. Soon the atom-bombs were dropped on Nagasaki and Hiroshima and the war with Japan ended in August 1945.

After all the years of suffering world war, it ended almost unexpectedly; within weeks soldiers started to return home. Though Carl came to England for 1945 Christmas, he promised to try to get back in March for the birth of our baby; he knew that he would soon be returning to America. Tony was home from the Marines for Christmas. He was walking with a cane after spending some time in a military hospital, recuperating from an injury from a parachute jump. We all had a good holiday together.

Carl got a long leave when our son, Philip, was born March 18, 1946 in Dartford Hospital. I was in hospital for two weeks (normal stay in those days) with Philip in a little cradle attached to the end of my bed. Carl and my mother visited as often as was allowed. By the time I was able to return home, his leave was up. He contacted the army authorities in London and they gave him a few days extension. We were all very proud of the baby and took him everywhere in his Silver Cross pram.

But Carl's time with the army was running out and he was shipped back to the States, discharged from the army and sent back to Oregon. He had been living in Oregon with his parents before being called to the army. During the more than four years that he served, his family had moved back to Missouri where he had lived as a child. They tried to convince him to also return, but he didn't want to go back to the mid-west. So he moved in with his brother, John, until he returned to England for Christmas 1946! He had missed us.

Philip wasn't old enough to travel as they had changed the rules. During and right after the war, GI war brides had been traveling with very small babies and many of whom had died in the troop ship surroundings. The regulation now said they had to be two years old to travel and though Carl tried to get me to make arrangements for the journey, I was reluctant to try. He was working for a painter and decorator in Salem and decided to save his money, get a passport and return to England for Christmas. He ended up working in England for over a year; the whole family was pleased and excited to have him with us again.

Once again we had a wonderful Christmas and, again, Carl helped us cut a tree, which he decorated with rigged-up lights and brought us fun food from America. In the New Year, he went to work for Bill Sissons, a contractor who lived at the end of our street, rebuilding bomb-damaged houses. Carl was very popular with all the neighbors; they always stopped to talk to him as he walked down the street. He caused excitement one Easter when he came to the house with a great big bunch of daffodils for me. The ladies across the street thought that was so romantic, and so did I!

This arrangement worked very well for a while but my brother, Tony, came out of the service because of his injured leg. Though he spent a lot of time at his girlfriend's house, he still needed a room in Ma's place. Geoffrey was growing up and the house we all shared was getting too small for the six of us. Houses were in great demand in those days.

Many people were living with several families in one home; all of our area had been badly bombed, and houses were damaged or destroyed. Also food was a big problem, very scarce. Carl was issued with a ration book, but we also had to find food. Ma and I would stand in line for hours to get our rations. At times, they would be out of supplies when we reached the head of the line. We heard of a shop in Dartford about five or six miles away that sold rabbits for one day each week; no ration coupons needed. We would ride the bus there and stand in line hoping they would still have some for sale by the time we reached the counter! Ma used to make good rabbit stew; carrots were not rationed but potatoes and onions were; bread, cakes and flour were severely rationed. Long lines of people queued up well before the bread was out of the oven with their bread units ready to exchange for the amount of bread allowed.

To help out financially, I got a job in a bakery, counting bread units received from customers to be traded for flour to make more bread. It was all a complicated, much-regulated system. I did receive an allowance for Philip and myself from the American government every month; it was so strange to me, as I did not know anything about checks or checking accounts.

Joy with Geoffrey, growing up in Bexleyheath
on Marlborough Road ~ 1945

Finally, others convinced me that I should go to America; the pressure was on. I would often hear: "Joy, you have to go to America; you have to follow your husband." Carl had certainly proven himself to be a responsible husband and father. The house was getting crowded with our family of three, my 13-year-old brother and Tony, coming home from the forces. I think my mother was a bit overwhelmed and wanted a little peace and quiet. She was often upset because she knew I would eventually leave, and she did not want me to go away. She had hoped I would be there to take care of her as she aged; many older women thought that was a daughter's duty and tried to keep them in the family home. It was not until years later I realized how alone I had left her. Maybe she already saw her future as a widow; her boys would marry and find work elsewhere and her daughter, living 5,000 miles away with her grandchildren, would never really be part of her life.

I had to go to the American Embassy in Grosvenor Square in London, the American Army Headquarters, to go through the channels and 'red tape' to get permission to travel to Oregon. As the wife of an American citizen and our son with both British and American birth certificates, our expenses were paid by the American Government. After applying and being interviewed by U.S. Army personnel and a chaplain, I was issued with 17 travel order copies, although no passport. Philip's name and picture were entered on Carl's American passport.

We packed our things in a big tin trunk and a couple of suitcases, though not very well or safely. We dismantled Philip's crib, which they would allow us to take. I was very sad that we couldn't take his beautiful pram (one of those royal looking English baby carriages) because of the wheels. What dummies we were. I later found out that the wheels could be removed and secured inside the pram and all put in a crate. I hated to lose that pram. How silly of me not to have learned more. We had some furniture, but it all had to stay behind.

I remember the morning in January 1948, when we left Southampton for our very long journey on a very small ship, the S.S. Marine Falcon. It was a Liberty ship that had been used during the war to convey troops and goods from America to Europe, traveling in convoy formation across the Atlantic. Philip looked so adorable in the lovely coat and legging sets with jaunty caps to match that Ma had made for him to wear on this journey to keep him warm. We had reins for him; something that was used for all English toddlers in those days. They were very valuable at sea as he wanted to run all over the ship. It was as if he had been at sea all his life. Although I had resisted leaving, the actual departure was exciting, just as stepping off into the unknown is exciting and scary at the same time.

The ship left Southampton with few passengers and very little in the hold, certainly not enough to provide ballast on a stormy ocean. We stopped in Cork, Ireland to pick up more passengers, who were brought out in a carrier that swung on a metal arm as the ship could not get close to the shore.

The Irish were hilarious, yet scary. They laughed a lot, drank a lot, and danced a lot on the deck. It was a very rough trip and many of them were seasick. But it bothered them very little; they were going to have a good time! They all had sleeping bunks in the hold and Carl was there too. He was shocked at their drunken behavior and also told me that they put their pajamas on over their suits for fear they might drown or not be properly dressed on the trip—or perhaps lose their new suits bought for life in America. They celebrated almost all night long, drinking and dancing every night of the trip. Years later when I saw the movie, 'Titanic,' the scenes of the passengers partying in the hold reminded me of those days on the 'Marine Falcon.'

It was on this ship that I first experienced resentment against blacks. A very polite, well-spoken nicely dressed man from Jamaica was traveling, and we enjoyed talking with him. He was a lawyer who had booked a ticket on a large ocean liner; I believe the Queen Mary. But on his arrival at the dock, he was refused passage because he was black. The only ship that would accept him was this one. We could tell from his conversation that it was devastating to be treated in that manner.

Philip and I were in a cabin with another GI bride from my hometown and with her two daughters. As a merchant ship, the men could not be in the cabins with the women; even married couples were separated as we traveled in a ship regulated by the government. The ship was small, very old and in poor repair, and the sea was very, very rough.

We found the Atlantic Ocean so overwhelmingly large: you could go for days seeing nothing but miles of grey sea; no life in sight in any direction seemed impossible. The sea was rough from the start. Water rushed through troughs on the deck and sometimes people forgot to close the waterproof doors to the inside corridors, allowing the water to rush in. For a couple of days, the captain turned south towards the

Azores for better weather and a little sunshine. Finally we had to turn back into the storms to reach New York Harbor.

During the trip we hit more severe weather, a tempest with high winds and driving rain. There were towering dark waves edged in white foamy froth (which our son reveled in watching, calling it soapy water), spilling over the ship and flooding the passages. The ship, which lacked ballast, finally rose on two waves and buckled in the middle—causing a split in the side of the hull! There were passengers with broken arms and legs caused by flying tables and chairs. Several large areas were cordoned off because of the danger. The water was running through all the ship's passageways, deep enough to soak our shoes. At meal times, you weren't sure whose plate of food was in front of you as the ship rolled so badly and the tables were often steeply slanted. Many of the passengers were ill and although Philip and I managed to escape seasickness, Carl did not fare so well.

We took 14 days instead of the promised ten to cross the Atlantic and arrived in New York Harbor too late to pick up a pilot to bring us into the dock. So, that first night was spent outside the harbor. The next morning, February 15, 1948, we sailed past the Statue of Liberty. So many people crowded the deck to see her, it was unbelievable! There were more than I had seen during the two-week trip; I think they must have been confined to their cabins the whole voyage! I vowed then that I would never cross the Atlantic again on anything other than a large, luxury, ocean-going liner with no more troop ships for me. So far, I have kept that promise I made to myself!

We went through customs on the ship. Ellis Island had been closed years before to arrivals and was used only for detainees: those not welcome in the country, experiencing problems in their homeland, or ill and possibly bringing in disease. Then we were taken to Fort Hamilton, an army base in Brooklyn, where my papers were checked, and I was processed into the United States of America. This was only after promising to be a good citizen, not become a prostitute and not plot to overthrow the U. S. Government!

We were there three days, sleeping in army cots and living in barracks. We were allowed two single beds and we pushed them together against the wall. Philip was to sleep next to the wall as we thought it would be the safest place for him. But during one night I woke up frantic; my baby was gone! We found that he had slipped between the bed and the wall and we thought we had lost him. We found him fast asleep under the bed safe and comfortable. One night we were able to go into the city. It was just after Valentine's Day and the stores had heart-shaped boxes of chocolates on sale and Carl bought me one. He was always good with gifts; years later he bought me a mixer for Father's Day saying, "Without you, I wouldn't be a father." Often when we were walking in London, he would buy little bunches of violets from the flower ladies stalls and pin them on my coat.

My impressions of New York were of tall buildings crowding out the daylight. Times Square seemed a strangely small area among the skyscrapers, not a place for celebrations as I had read in magazines. The storm at sea had raised havoc on land too with a tremendous snowstorm. Snow had been swept from the sidewalks and piled very high in the gutters, dirty and full of garbage. It was certainly not the glamorous place I had imagined; already London was better! I was really disillusioned by Times Square. Crowds of people on the sidewalks kicking snow; underground trains with basket weave seats and you had to go above ground to change lines. It was nothing like the elegant London tube with its upholstered seats where railway lines connected in all directions without the need to leave the tunnels. We rode it through Brooklyn to Fort Hamilton. After wandering around New York, Brooklyn and Fort Hamilton for three days and not being particularly impressed with anything (certainly not finding gold-paved streets as so many soldiers had spoken of, and certainly not the glamorous big city I had read about), I wondered if all immigrants had thought the same on their arrival.

We rode the train to Chicago where we changed to the train for Oregon. As we had to wait all afternoon, we thought we'd take a walk. But out of the station we turned the corner and the wind was so strong we couldn't walk in it; we gave up and stayed inside the station. No wonder they call it the 'Windy City.' We were several days on the train which was called either, 'The City of Portland' or the 'Portland Rose,' both ran that route and, at this time, I cannot remember which train we were riding. It seemed as if all the interesting countryside was passed through after dark; we saw lots of Wyoming in daylight.

We had almost no money so we bought very little food. One evening Carl encouraged me to order a salad, oh my! In England a salad was a couple of pieces of lettuce, a slice or two of beetroot and tomato with a little dab of salad cream. This was a great bowl of salad greens with all the toppings, a chef's salad. I could hardly eat it all. We left the train at Portland after traveling alongside the Columbia River's wonderful scenery which was more exciting than earlier parts of the journey. Then we transferred to a Greyhound bus to ride down the old 99E highway to Salem through Oregon City, Canby, Hubbard and Woodburn, with streets scattered with businesses and run-down buildings.

We were to stay with Carl's brother, John, so we went to his house on Broadway and only his wife Lucille was there. John had gone to the Salem railway station thinking we would end our journey there. We all greeted each other and laughed at this mistake; we stayed there at 1945 Broadway NE for a month and slept on the living room couch. Carl went to work immediately with a painter he had worked with before he had returned to England, and soon the Teamsters demanded he join the union. We didn't have the money for dues so he had to find non-union work.

After a month with John and Lucille we moved to a motel in the Hollywood North Salem district. Housing was difficult to find; so many men were coming back from the services, getting married and wanting to find homes. Hollywood district was at the junction of North Capitol and Fairgrounds Road. The Hollywood theatre was across from the motel and there were several small shops including Slim Hale's jewelry shop. Slim's wife, Kay, was very friendly. She was expecting a baby and invited me to her baby shower, a new experience for me as we didn't have baby showers in England. Later that year, she hosted one for me. We lost touch but 20 years after, my middle daughter, Barbara, married her only child, Frank!

It was nice being just the three of us but I was very homesick. Carl went to work each day and I had little to do. The rain bothered me a lot. I came here at the time of the Vanport floods in Portland when whole streets of houses were washed away. Keizer was also flooded at the time and the news of the disaster reached my family; they were worried that I was living in a bad area.

Carl's brother, Edgar showed up at my door one day unexpectedly and it was great to meet him. I was comfortable, even though Carl was working, as I recognized him from his picture. He visited for three days and was easy to talk to. He took me to the restaurant next door to the motel and bought me my first hamburger. I had mixed feelings about it. I had never tasted meat ground that way; it felt funny on my tongue.

We spent a lot of time with John and Lucille and their children, Fred and Esther. But to John I was always a foreigner and he tried to teach me to be an American. He and I had the same initials and both signed our names J. A. Beebe. He told me he was known that way in Salem and I would have to change my signature. So to keep the peace, I have been known as Joy A. Beebe ever since. Not a drastic problem just a little disconcerting at the time. He was very unsympathetic about my life during the war, even though Carl tried to explain how difficult things had been for the English. John meant well but I was too torn up with the changes in my life to respond well.

We had arrived in Salem with only $10. Most of our luggage had been broken or spoiled in the storm at sea; we really had nothing except our clothes and our little son. All the changes were not easy to handle, and I was unsure that my first real travel adventure had been a success.

Chapter Eight

A NEW COUNTRY, A NEW LIFE

It was not easy to come from London to Salem; the contrast was amazing. I had come from the suburbs of one of the biggest cities in the world and Salem seemed to be nothing but a village. The whole downtown shopping area could be walked in just a few minutes. Cherry Avenue was a gravel road. I would ride the bus from Keizer to Salem from the few large houses on River Road through the open fields, where the Northwest Natural Gas Company and Fred Meyers have since been built. I would be surprised when I rode the bus; it seemed like the passengers spoke just like the actors I had seen in the American movies. One lady called me "'Darling" each time she saw me, yet nothing else even remotely resembled the movies, houses, churches or shops.

My mother didn't write for several months; did I wish I hadn't come? I'm sure I did. After a month in the motel, we found a two-bedroom house to rent in Keizer. We had shipped Philip's cot from England and bought a double bed, a kitchen table and chairs, hot-plate to cook on and got a refrigerator on a payment plan, also something new to me. Later Carl found me an antique cook stove. It was an electric one on legs with an oven on the side. The living room and the second bedroom were totally empty for over a year. All my dishes, except one platter, had been broken during the storm when we were on the ship. I cried and cried and sometimes was completely hysterical. But there was no way out; I had to learn to go forward. Carl was always kind, rarely said a cross word; he completely understood my sadness. I expect he too had been homesick when he left for the Army. Really, there's nothing one can do except carry on and make the best of things.

The first Christmas was difficult though Carl made it as nice as he could. We had two children by then. Jennifer Joy was born November 9, 1948, on a very foggy night. My mind was on England and I kept remembering that day was Lord Mayor's Show Day in London. We had bought an older model car by then and that night Cherry Avenue was so dark (the fog rising from the standing water north of the Oregon Deaf School) that Carl stood on the running board with the driver's door open, leaning out to see where he was driving. I remember the sound of frogs croaking as they hopped across the road.

Carl got paid for a job on Christmas Eve. He wanted to buy me a gift and started for Salem but it was snowing hard and he could only get as far as the junction of River Road and Cherry Avenue. Luckily, a hardware store, Coomler and Franz, was at the junction where he bought a blue teapot for me; a gift I have treasured all these years. He also went to do some shopping at a little store on Cherry Avenue and bought a raffle ticket; how lucky, he won a turkey! Lucille cooked it for us as we had no oven at that time. It all helped to make things more festive although it took me years to really feel at home. I was often bothered by loud noises and by airplanes flying over, reminiscent of air raids and explosions during the war. Carl said I would become white and very nervous when hearing planes.

When John and Lucille came to play cards or board games, they brought their card table and we carried the chairs from the kitchen into the living room, just to say we used the living room. Once we got an oven, I then managed to bake good cakes to serve at our card games. We had neighbors, married couples, Alice and Jimmy and Lurene and Elliot, who would play cards with us too. Soon I met other English war brides and we formed a club. In 1949, we voted to call ourselves the 'Accent Club;' it seemed fitting with the different languages and different accents: English, French, German, Australians, New Zealanders, Yugoslavians, and South Sea Islanders (Samoa). We still meet now, over 60 years later!

Often Carl and I would put our children into a turquoise-colored American style baby buggy that we bought from Hogg Bros in Salem and walk to John and Lucille's on Broadway or to downtown Salem. Keizer at that time was a suburb of Salem with quite a lot of open fields between the two towns. It finally became its own city in 1982. There were just a few shops and a grade school around Keizer Corners, the corner of North River Road and Chemawa Road. North River Road was lined with big old houses which today have mostly been razed and businesses built in their place. It was necessary to go into Salem to shop for any major item or find a super market. One thing we did enjoy was going to baseball games, watching the Salem Senators play in the ballpark at Mission Street and 25th in Salem. Sadly, it burned down in the 1960s. Occasionally, we would go to the pictures (see a movie), but that meant a babysitter, which added to the cost of a night out.

Years later, Carl and I decided to learn to dance, so with Fred and Olive (an English couple with whom we were friends) we took lessons and sometimes went to night clubs in Portland to dance. Once, Carl and I won a prize at Piluso's Club in Portland in a waltz competition! I was wearing a white knit dress with a satin lining, which absolutely glowed under the black-light highlighting the dance floor.

One day in early 1950, I walked up to the Cupboard Drive-Inn (restaurant) at the end of the street and asked for a job. I had no experience and was not even good at counting American money or understanding colloquial expressions. Surprisingly, I was given one! I worked evenings and so started my restaurant career. Carl stayed with the children and was working on building a house for us.

One day he was working on the roof when Jennifer, not yet two years old, surprised him with a "Hello Daddy," poking her head over the top. He was so shocked! She had climbed the ladder to the top of the roof. He was a painter but it was a very seasonal job. Though he tried very hard to get something more reliable, he always went back to painting when the weather improved in the spring.

Jennifer by our family car, years before I learned to drive

On March 17, 1951, our daughter, Barbara Anne, was born. She didn't even wait for the doctor to arrive. In those days the cost for the baby doctor was $100; as he wasn't there, he took $25 off the bill! The nurse reminded me it was St. Patrick's Day but not being in the best frame of mind I told her I was English, not Irish! The memory is a grim reminder of how I sometimes say the wrong thing! Luckily, a friend and I had given a birthday party for my son, Philip, that day; though his birthday was not until the following day. Otherwise, he would not have had a celebration.

Our fourth child, Vivian Elaine was born March 4, 1953, so we had three birthdays in March. She was smallest of my four children. Within her first year, her baby photo was entered in a contest and won a prize. I kept on with my waitress jobs and eventually became a restaurant owner, so far from the career I had dreamed of so long ago.

We moved house several times; once because the house we were living in caught fire. We did not understand that the fire department had condemned it (the owner did not disclose it) and after the firemen left, we continued to live in it. A month later, it caught fire again! It had a faulty flue from the oil stove and we were told by the fireman to leave immediately. We found it difficult to find another house as it was New Year's Day.

At that time we had three children, and it had been devastating to try to move the little ones out of the house to the neighbors and then call the fire department; Carl was not home at the time. I was panicking, having remembered fires during the bombing raids in England; Jennifer has never lost her fear of fire since then. We were always renting until Carl received his Oregon Veterans bonus in 1952 and we bought a small house on Bailey Road in Keizer.

Carl and Joy with Barbara, Jennifer, Philip, Vivian in 1957

We were happy in that little house and lived there for five years. Vivian was born when we lived there and John came to sit with Philip, Jennifer and Barbara while Carl took me to the hospital. In time our house grew too small, with four children and Carl's brother, Edgar, staying with us. He had been discharged out of the U.S. Army that he had been required to join; his service in the Merchant Marines during the war years did not count as conscription service. He had married in Japan and was waiting to go back to Japan and bring his wife, Chizuko, to America. Carl's sister, Betty, stayed with us too after she had graduated from High School in Eldorado Springs, Missouri, as she wanted to find a job in Oregon.

We were wondering how we could manage to get a bigger place when, one evening, the neighbors (the people who had sold the house to us) knocked on the door and offered to buy the property back for more than we paid for it. It was a corner of their acreage and they wanted to reconnect it. We were happy to say yes.

It was July 1957, and I spent the next few weeks looking for another house to buy and was disappointed to find how high prices were. Time was getting short when Carl came home from work one day with a prospect. The builder, for whom he was painting, was building a new house for his family and quoted a price on the one they were leaving, that he had also built, and offered to carry the mortgage. It wasn't what I wanted, but Carl put his foot down and said it was a well-built house at a price we could handle. They moved in 30 days, though their new house was not finished, and we started to move once again. I vowed then that I would never move house again. I had come many miles across the ocean and the United States of America and seemed to be constantly unsettled. Thankfully, I have been in the same house 55 years this September.

My children, Vivian, Jennifer, Barbara, Philip ~ 1957

Our new address was 782 Sunset Avenue though later changed to 390 when they renumbered the street from River Road to the west. Barbara was to start the first grade at Cummings school, and each afternoon when I picked her up from school we moved boxes to the new house. She was tremendously excited about being the first of the family to see our new home, and she has enjoyed it ever since. I really was not happy with it at first, mainly because it was so much darker than our previous one. It had only one large picture window in the living-room. There had been windows on two sides on Bailey Road and the painted walls on Sunset Avenue were all dark, even in the kitchen and bedrooms. Carl, being a painter, promised that could be easily changed though it did take long time.

Through the years, we have added and remodeled, and now I love it; I hope to live here for the rest of my days. Carl added a dining room when I was vacationing with my family in England in the late 1970s and surprised me by having it 90 percent done when I got home! In 1973, we had a swimming pool installed in the back yard. Later we added a solarium, a beautiful room full of windows and facing south getting lots of sun and always lovely to sit in and relax. The house sits on almost half an acre and the back garden, after years of care, is lovely to look at through the large south facing windows. So, Carl was right in 1957 when he told me it was the house for us, and we could make it into a place we would enjoy.

There were excellent schools close by for the girls to attend. Philip went to Keizer school in 1952, which has now been moved several blocks from its original site and later restored and renamed Keizer Heritage Center, promoting Keizer history. He graduated from North Salem High School, as there was not a high school open in Keizer until Jennifer's graduation year, 1966. Our short street leads down to the Willamette River and a small park. It has been, so far, a safe and friendly neighborhood. Many families have lived here almost as long as I have and until recently, some even longer.

River Road, the main road leading into Salem is now a four-lane road; there is close access to the freeway for points north and south of Salem. New schools have been built and many stores and super markets. In 1982, Keizer became a city, with its own police force, fire department and city hall. Every May, for over 50 years, and even before it was incorporated as a city, Keizer has celebrated its Iris Festival with a parade and entertainment lasting three days. The Iris flower is commemorated as it is widely grown in the area and plants are shipped from Keizer iris farms all over the world. Through the years my children, grandchildren and great-grandchildren have been participants in the parade; it has all been a lot of fun.

Parts of Keizer have flooded badly through the years yet I have been lucky; my home is situated at the top of a rise about two blocks from the river. Although I have seen several bad floods in the area, it has not reached my home.

I traveled with the family around Oregon, Idaho and Washington by car during those years. I took the Greyhound bus once to see Farrol, my friend in California. Another time I went to Vancouver, Canada, with some girls I worked with, one of whom had relatives living in a nearby Vancouver suburb.

During my years in America I had seen very little of Carl's parents, Opal and Roy Beebe. They came to Salem in May 1957 for their daughter

Betty's wedding; I think they had only visited one other time before that. Then Roy, Carl's dad, died in October 1957, and his mother came to live in Dallas, Oregon for a few years to be near her brother, Menefee. Menefee died in the late 1960s, and my mother-in-law returned to Eldorado Springs, Missouri. I remember her staying with us for the Christmas holidays one year. Vivian wanted a piano and we had bought a secondhand one for her Christmas gift. Carl and I were awakened about 3:30 a.m. Christmas morning with the sounds of loud piano playing; Grandma Opal was entertaining our four children with Christmas Carols! Although instruments were not allowed in her church, she initially learned to play the organ and later the piano. She played most of her life and was having fun with the children.

Carl and I flew to Missouri to see her in 1971 when she was in hospital. We landed in Kansas City, rented a car and saw fabulous brick homes on wide streets. I had not seen big brick mansions in large sculptured gardens since I had left England and was very impressed. Things were very different when we reached the small town of Eldorado Springs, where Carl's mother lived. I don't believe there was even one house with an attached garage; they all looked so small, dingy and rundown.

The shops were small family businesses: little cafes, no supermarket (we didn't find one) and the only motel was outside the town. While we were waiting for the reception clerk to figure out whether he had a room for rent or not, cockroaches were walking across his desk. Carl said "Forget it," and "we've decided to move on." It was about 30 miles to the next motel, and we drove back and forth each time we visited the hospital. There were no liquor stores, nor was liquor served in restaurants but you could buy it in service stations!

By the time we left, I could understand why Carl liked Oregon better. We never went back to Missouri as Carl's mother, Lillian Opal Riley Beebe, died on February 1, 1972—her 72nd birthday and the 55th anniversary of her wedding day!

We used to take our family on Sunday drives. It was not until years later I learned they didn't think it was much fun to crowd into the back seat of the car and go where their parents chose, although they enjoyed the stops for ice cream in Silverton or hamburgers at Bob's 19 cent hamburgers. Vivian tells me they did enjoy going places, eating ice cream, etc.; they just didn't want to be crowded in the back seat with each other. I think they enjoyed the few trips we made to the snowy mountains where they learned to ski or to the coast to play on the beach and get wet.

Roy and Opal Beebe, on their wedding day ~
February 1, 1917

One of our favorite places to go was Seattle to visit Carl's brother, Edgar. We would take our boat up to Seattle and put it in the water on Puget Sound or go across to Blake Island; it was a holiday for all of us. Edgar's Japanese wife, Chizuko, and dog Poochie, always came along. On the islands we would collect clams and in the bay, where the water was so clear you could see the bottom, and we would fish for flat fish, like flounder. They would lie on the bottom, and you could dangle the bait in front of them and watch them snap at it and be caught. I doubt a true fisherman would think it very sporting. Once our outboard motor would not start on the return trip from the island and we had to travel a long distance back with a two and a half horsepower-trolling engine. A long trip, especially as the tank had to be filled with gas frequently and Chizuko was sitting alongside it, smoking a cigarette! Imagine how nerve-racking that would be!

We were there the year of the Seattle World's Fair and spent time riding up the Space Needle and checking out the exhibits. We enjoyed going to the locks to watch the boats rise in the water and when the lock gates opened, the boats would go on their way. The steep hilly streets of downtown Seattle and Pike's Market were fun too. We would shop in the Japanese store near the train station for trinkets and paper-wrapped candy; the paper was edible and the kids loved it and always wanted to return for more!

Chizuko was a great cook; we so enjoyed her battered deep-fried fish called Tempura; we consumed it faster than she could cook it. Sadly, Chizuko died young; I never really knew how old she was. She was a victim of the atom-bomb dropped on Nagasaki, Japan, at the end of World War II. She had several cancer operations before she left Japan in 1956 and was often in ill health. She was fun company even though she spoke very little English. A few years later, Edgar remarried and we enjoyed visiting with his new wife, Bonnie, checking out the remodeling job he did on the house, especially the basement play room. Edgar died about 1997; Bonnie and her daughter moved to Missouri and we lost contact.

Chapter Nine

RETURNING TO 'THE OLD COUNTRY'

In February 1968, I made my first trip back to England, exactly 20 years after my arrival in New York, U.S.A. I flew on a Pan Am Boeing 707; it was one of the best flights I ever had. The plane wasn't crowded, the food was excellent, traveling through the sunset was a thrill, and there were no stops on the flying route over the North Pole. I traveled Pan Am several times, and it was the best airline I ever flew. It's such a pity they were ruined by a terrible disaster in December 1988, when the flight from London to New York was blown up in a deadly terrorist attack as it passed over Lockerbie, Scotland. Mismanagement, other disasters and multi-million dollar law suits ended with the dissolution of Pan Am Airlines. They had been the best in the business since the 1927.

My mother had been writing sad letters believing that she might soon die, so I took three weeks off from work and went to see her. She was living in Erith, a London suburb on the River Thames, in one of those awful grey cement tower blocks that England built after World War II, housing families that had been bombed-out during the air raids.

Ma and Joy in Erith, Kent Apartment ~ 1968

They were rather grim looking, about ten stories high and smelled heavily of disinfectant inside. The halls and elevators were dirty and had trash lying in the corners and junk on the stairs. But once the apartment entrance door was closed, there was a nice, clean and cozy bed-sitting room with a small kitchen and a bathroom. The kind lady, 'the warden' (I never knew her by any other name), who was on call in case Ma had any problems, found a folding cot for me, and I slept across the living room from Ma.

Ma seemed demanding, wanting me to be with her all the time. But so many years had passed, and we were like strangers to each other having very little to talk about. I wondered, 'Did we ever have long talks together?' I don't remember us ever being close, and she did not want to hear about my life in America. Her sister, Alice Therin, came to visit, and Mother was quite upset that we went out together; Ma felt I should stay home with her. We invited her to come shopping with us or to a restaurant, but she was not willing. She did like to play the invalid, and I suppose I should have been more considerate. She also had always been a little jealous of Alice, a sister who had never married, traveled to foreign countries, and (I believe) had the kind of life that Ma wanted.

Ma encouraged me to go to Bexleyheath, where I had lived for so long before I went to America, and to visit Hall Place in Bexley where Carl had been stationed during the war. She wanted to know how much things had changed. It was interesting to see how many of the shops I had known had survived. The Regal cinema was a gambling hall now, but the ice cream store next door to it was still there, serving parfaits and 'Knickerbocker Glory's,' a tall glass filled with a wonderful mix of fruit, ice cream and whipped cream. The bomb-damaged dry cleaners and grocery shops had been rebuilt. Hyde's department store was an attractive store with far more goods than it had sold in the war years. Boots Chemist had been modernized; I didn't know then that my cousin Betty worked there; what fun it would have been to say hello to her! Yet the parking in Townley Road, the Clock Tower and the many buses were all much the same.

Though new arterial roads had been built around Hall Place, the U.S. Army guardhouse (where I used to meet Carl) still stood at the entrance. The gardens had been restored to their former beauty and the Black Prince pub was encircled with a ring road, making it difficult to enter without a car. The main thing I noticed was the number of Pakistanis in the area. There had been political troubles between India and Pakistan and many of them had come to live in England to escape the riots. As colonials, they had a form of British passport and had no trouble entering the country, where the women continued to wear their traditional saris and head veils and the men, turbans. It was strange to see bus drivers wearing turbans.

Although Ma had visited me in Salem in 1963, she still did not accept that things were better for me in America than they would have been in England; I was still her daughter and should be taking care of her.

When she came to America she had flown via Canada into Seattle, and I drove her to my home from there. She was amazed at the wide-open countryside each side of the freeway and also pleased with having flown over the Rocky Mountains. Carl would take us for Sunday drives into the mountains of Eastern Oregon and to the coast, where she put her feet into the Pacific Ocean. I think she enjoyed going places and eating out, but even though she was only 69, she would tire easily. We had fixed up a small room behind our garage for Carl and me so that she could have our master bedroom during her stay. She had come to visit with a four-year visa, but after four months she wanted to return home. Geoffrey's wife, Brenda, wrote to say her mother had died, and Ma was afraid she herself would die in a foreign country. She had always been a 'stay-at-home mother' so she was probably not very happy with me. I had to go to work at least five days a week in a restaurant and, of course, four children in the house made it noisier than she was accustomed to. Several of my English friends came to visit, but it was too much for her; I believe she had lived alone quietly for too long.

And now back to my 1968 trip to England. Geoffrey was living on the Isle of Wight off the coast of England with his wife, Brenda, and two daughters, Julie and Sonia, and Ma suggested I go there for a few days visit. I took the train from London to Southampton and the ferry across to the island where I met the family for the first time. I enjoyed the wonderful tour they gave me of the all the interesting and historic spots on the island. It was such a cold February; I practically froze to death. Actually I had expected England to be covered in snow as I remembered February had always been a snowy month when I lived there. I had even brought my boots to be prepared, but there was no snow; the weather was just very cold and dry.

Geoffrey and Brenda took me completely around the coastline of the island, visiting small villages of thatched roof houses with interesting churches and the Blackgang Chine, an old haunt of smugglers. Only open to visitors in the summer, we passed on visiting Osborne House, the 19th century residence of Queen Victoria and Prince Albert. We walked along the beach in Cowes, where the Royal Yacht Regatta is held in the summer every year. All wonderful and new to me; I had never been there before. They were great hosts and I had a lovely time and talked about coming back with my family.

Now, it was time to spend a few more days with Ma. So after a long weekend with them, I went back to Erith before returning home. I was pleasantly surprised when Geoffrey came up on the train on my last day. He was so pleased to see me, his big sister again. Sadly, I needed to return to America. I missed my family, my home and hopefully, they were missing me.

I had been surprised by the depressed attitude of many of the working people in England: no smiles or greetings from neighbors, shop girls or paper boys any more. Many things had not properly recovered from the war. A great deal of labour and money had gone into rebuilding European countries (including Germany) and the English were upset, even resentful. It had been over 20 years since the war's end, yet many bombed areas had not been rebuilt. Shoddy goods were in the stores and people felt there was an increasing gap between the classes. Many waitresses or shop workers seemed unhappy in their jobs.

Chapter Ten

THE HIGHLIGHT OF MY VISIT WAS THE DAY I WENT BACK TO LONDON

I was truly excited! I was going to spend a day in London on my own. Nothing could have pleased me more. About the middle of my three-week stay, I took the crowded train from the local station in Erith to London Bridge Station, the way I had taken to work every day as a teenager. I was so confident, so happy. I was in London, My Town! My feet never faltered; boldly retracing paths I had so often traveled 20 years earlier.

Leaving the station, I walked across the bridge (London Bridge, not Tower Bridge) with its crowds of people rushing to their jobs. Bicycles, cars, lorries, and double-decker buses were going each way with garbage, empty cigarette packs and newspapers all tumbling in the wind. Just as it had always been, the broad shining river flowed beneath this setting. At the far end, I stopped and looked over the heavy cement railing down into the Billingsgate Fish Market, below on the bank of the River Thames. Dozens of men rushing around wearing flat-topped leather hats, carrying large fish or boxes of fish on their heads— stalls of fish,

fish everywhere with trucks loading, men yelling and shouting and water sloshing on the display carts and the road; it was wonderful.

They go to work in the early morning hours, boats filled with fish line up at the wharf; the noisy job of selling fish keeps going on for hours. Fish is delivered all over England from that market and has been for centuries.

Tower Bridge, London

The view of the River Thames and Tower Bridge was enchanting with very special and wonderful memories. Oh, how I have loved London; the action and rush of a big city. I was back in England, yet I knew in my mind that my home and family were calling me back to America. Still, I'll never forget the excitement of London that I knew as a young girl.

The Monument to the Great Fire of London in the 1600's still stood proudly in the centre of the market, on the spot where the Great Fire had started 300 years before. It had even escaped bomb damage from the World War II though much of the surrounding city had been destroyed. I walked on through the city, down Moorgate to Finsbury Square and to the building where I started my first paying job with the Inland Revenue Service. Later I walked to the Tower of London across from the Port of London Authority building, which held another tax office I worked in during the early 1940s. I never once got lost or turned a wrong corner.

When I worked there, Carl would ride the train in early and during my lunch hour we would walk in the gardens of the Tower of London and plan our wedding, our future. The gardens surrounding the Tower were planted in the area that was the moat in past centuries where they dumped refuse, worthless rubbish, bodies of hanged criminals and traitors—the severed heads were put on spikes on London Bridge. I have always enjoyed the Tower of London; it's one of the greatest places in London with its history dating back over 900 years.

The Beefeaters, in their picturesque uniform, keep the visitors intrigued with stories from its bloody history. There are 'rooks,' large black birds, strutting around on the grassy areas. It is said that if the rooks ever leave the Tower, Britain will fall! So far, they seem to be happy where they enjoy the crowds of people wandering around the ancient tower built by William the Conqueror in the 11th century. Before World War II, the crown jewels were displayed there and one had to climb up a very narrow stone spiral staircase to view them. Now they are in a much more modern setting.

My grandfather, William Thomas Beaver, was with the Metropolitan Police. He wore the navy blue policeman's uniform with the tall helmet. This is not the Elizabethan costume of the Yeoman of the Guard, commonly known as Beefeaters (he was a Bobby, not a Beefeater), and for many years his beat was inside the Tower of London. A story has been told that he once dived into the River Thames and rescued a man from drowning. He lived with his family on Tower Hill until he retired in 1919. Since then, the houses have been torn down. I believe this is why I have such a strong feeling of interest in the Tower. I enjoy it more than any other castle I have ever visited. Its history is awe inspiring.

Tower of London, Traitors' Gate

The Tower of London is right on the River Thames. In past centuries, prisoners were brought down the river in open boats, entered through Traitor's Gate and taken to their prison cells. Among the most famous was Anne Boleyn, second wife of Henry VIII, beheaded on the Block on the Tower Green. Princess Elizabeth, daughter of Henry VIII and Anne Boleyn, was brought through Traitor's Gate. This occurred during the reign of her half sister, Mary Tudor, oldest and only child of Henry VIII and Katherine of Aragon, his first queen. Mary was a devout Catholic who was afraid the people of England favored the protestant religion at that time and would rebel and supplant her with Elizabeth. I believe that Elizabeth was one of the few who lived to leave the Tower, after entering it as a prisoner through Traitor's Gate; she resumed her life and became the most famous Queen of England.

The block where prisoners were beheaded and the Church behind it are still there for visitors to see. This is the Tower where the two little princes were murdered in the 15th century. Though it was never proved, it is believed their Uncle Richard III, who ascended the throne in the place of the oldest prince (Edward), killed them.

Sir Walter Raleigh, who traveled to America in the 1500's and introduced tobacco to Europe, was imprisoned twice—once by Queen Elizabeth and later by James I. Raleigh wrote books while there, explored the Americas between prison sentences and was eventually beheaded. The last prisoner in the Tower was Rudolph Hess, Adolf Hitler's Deputy, who flew to England during World War II with the idea of negotiating peace between England and Germany. The British government thought the Tower of London was the best place to imprison him until the end of the war, when he was tried in Nuremburg, Germany. The Russians kept him in prison for many years, and he died at 93, some say by his own hand.

Stories like this have always made it the most interesting and exciting place to visit. Nearby the Tower is the well-known Tower Bridge, built in the gothic style during Queen Victoria's long reign (18371901), 64 years. I walked to the West End of London where there were many historic theatres and high-class shops. I hailed a taxi and asked the driver to just drive me around to some of the wonderful places I remembered. He did well, like a regular tour guide. He had many stories and anecdotes to tell of the area. New office blocks were being built with lots of glass and many of Christopher Wren's churches, gutted during the war, were now tidied up but only as shells of the original building. There were still large open areas where buildings had been totally destroyed. The theatre district was as busy as ever, with lots of famous actors appearing in the plays. We drove around the large beautiful parks that are one of the peaceful additions to London. I told my mother how interesting the ride was, and she couldn't believe it when I told her he only charged me one pound!

I was so happy to be back in London that day in 1968 and happy to have discovered how easy it was to make the 5,000 mile flight from Oregon. I promised myself I would bring my children to see the country of my childhood and share my love of London history.

Chapter Eleven

RETURN TO ENGLAND WITH MY DAUGHTERS

S ummer 1969, I had now lived in Oregon for over 21 years. My son had signed up with the U. S. Navy during his final year in high school and had been overseas on and off ever since. My daughter, Jennifer, had married in July and was in her own home. Barbara had graduated high school at the end of May and was planning in the fall to go to Oregon State University (Oregon State College when I first came to America). Vivian still had two more years of high school before graduating. Somehow it seemed like a good time to take my two younger daughters to England.

We planned to visit with my mother in Erith, a town that is part of the Greater London Area right on the River Thames. We also planned to spend time on the Isle of Wight with my brother Geoffrey, his wife Brenda and two daughters Julie and Sonia, who were younger than my girls Barbara and Vivian. As a gift, each of my girls picked a shorts-and-top outfit for themselves and then bought one in the same design but a smaller size for their cousins. They had a good time being dressed alike.

For the early part of the trip, we were very lucky in finding rooms in The Running Horses; a pub close to my mother's flat, as her place was not large enough to accommodate all of us. Pubs often have rooms for travelers as well as bars and areas for families. The owners of the pub were on vacation and had left their teenage children to take care of running the business; they had been told not to take on any new guests while their parents were gone. But they immediately formed a bond with my girls and agreed to let us stay. Anne, Susan and Peter Wilson were lots of fun.

Vivian, Joy, Barbara at the Running Horses Pub ~ 1969

We had a wonderful time staying in the pub; the girls went on several trips with them and even helped with chores in the pub. I was invited to join them on a trip to the family summer home at Battle, near Hastings on the coast of Kent, to visit with the parents and have afternoon tea in the garden. Battle is an area in England that features importantly in English history. In 1066, William, Duke of Normandy, crossed the English Channel from France—the last successful invasion of Britain—to stake his claim to the throne of England, held at the time by King Harold. In the battle of Battle, King Harold was killed, shot in the eye with an arrow fired by William. William claimed the throne as William the Conqueror and from him all present British Royalty descends in a direct line. He built Windsor Castle and the Tower of London which are both still standing and lived in today. This historic story is recorded on a 70-meter long tapestry, known as the Bayeux tapestry, displayed in Bayeux, France. It was first displayed on July 14, 1077 and legend has it that Queen Mathilda of England (wife of William) and her ladies in-waiting, embroidered it.

The Running Horses, Erith, Kent ~ 1969

We traveled by train to Southampton and then took the ferry to the Isle of Wight, where Geoffrey met us all. Geoffrey drove us everywhere! English roads were now wider, modern motorways and crowded with cars, a lot different to the war time years. During our stay there we did a complete tour of the Island. There was much open countryside, rolling downs, with cows and sheep grazing peacefully and ocean vistas from the many stops we made; a favorite was The Needles, very tall pointed rocks jutting upward from the sea on the coastline. It was summertime and we were able to watch the yachts sailing around the island, some of them racing while others were cruising over to France across the English Channel. We spent hours enjoying the quaint thatched-roof villages, old country churches, a miniature village and many seaside towns with boats and sandy beaches. In Godshill, the church is high on a steep hill overlooking the village of thatched cottages. Legend has it that the church was to have been built lower in the village; but every morning when the workmen arrived at the site, the building stones had been moved to the top of a nearby hill. After weeks of this, no one knowing who was moving them, the workmen decided it must be God demanding the church be above the village. So they stopped returning the materials and built the church where God wanted it. There were no more problems; the church sits overlooking the village to this day.

Barbara, Vivian, Julie, Brenda, Sonia, Joy on the Isle of Wight ~ 1969

The girls went to the sheepdog trials and a Girl Guide camp with Julie, swam in the warm sea, played on the sandy but crowded beaches—trying to be modest when putting on their swim suits right there on the beach. They giggled and laughed trying to cover up in their large beach towels surrounded by the crowds of family gatherings. We had picnics and one day Barbara and Sonia (or was it Julie?) went to get ice cream cones leaving the rest of us sitting on the sandy beach. The tide was coming in so the group had to move closer to the wall. By the time the two girls found us they had eaten all the ice cream cones! Their excuse—they were melting!

We ate fish and chips nearby in the village of Carisbrooke, to repeat a lovely but unexpected dinner that I so much enjoyed the previous year. One evening during the 1968 visit, a casserole dish broke as Brenda was taking it from the oven. With our dinner splashed on the floor, Brenda quite calmly said, "Joy, did you say you wanted to take us out to dinner?" So, on this trip I wanted to take my girls to the same place we had eaten after the casserole disaster!

Our hosts took us to Carisbrooke Castle, where Charles I of England hid from Oliver Cromwell in 1646, before his beheading in the Banqueting Hall in Whitehall, London, in 1649. He had tried to escape but got stuck in a window, as he was larger than the opening. Charles

I had dissolved Parliament because the members would not approve of his requests or his religious theories. He had ruled as a dictator until he lost the Civil War, after which Oliver Cromwell (winning leader of the enemy party) became the Lord Protector of England and ruled for ten years. When Cromwell died, his son succeeded him but was not a good ruler. Eventually Charles II, son of the beheaded monarch, became King and the royal line of succession has continued unbroken since.

We stayed in London for three days; my Aunt Alice joined us at our fancy hotel in Knightsbridge, close to Harrods large department store. Harrods is a very elegant place with the fabulous Food Hall and remarkable artistic meat and fish display. We did all the touristy things one does in London: Westminster Abbey, Tower of London, St Paul's Cathedral, Pall Mall, Changing of the Guard at Whitehall and Buckingham Palace, etc. We had a marvelous time.

My Auntie Alice, Barbara, Vivian in London ~ 1969

Barbara was able to take her first trip to France, solo on the boat train from London to Dover, ferry to Boulogne on the coast of France, figuring out all the details on her own. We truly enjoyed everything we did! My girls were excited to meet new relatives and make new friends with

Anne, Susan and Peter from the Running Horses Pub—a friendship that has lasted through the years—and to learn how much fun traveling can be. They have both been back many times and also have an interest in exploring the world. At that time flying seemed easy and comfortable, but now crowds and security have made it more difficult.

Chapter Twelve

MY VISITS EXTEND TO OTHER COUNTRIES

M y mother died in January 1978, a few days before her 84th birthday. She had spent many years in care homes and at the end in hospital. She had difficulty walking for years and refused to try or even go anywhere by car. She had visited me in Salem in 1963 and was always proud that she had traveled to America. She would tell about her trip to the others in the various senior homes she stayed in during her later years, especially mentioning the mountains in Canada and America.

From 1968 until she died, I went back to see her once a year and several times Carl went with me. Sometimes I would take a friend and show them the places I loved in London. We would also take coach trips to Shakespeare country, Stratford-Upon-Avon, Warwick Castle, Bath, Oxford, Tewksbury and of course, the Isle of Wight with old castles, manor houses, famous cathedrals, all places I had never visited when I lived in England. I certainly learned more about England after I no longer lived there.

On one of my first visits to England I learned that my brother, Tony, had remarried in 1969. He and his new wife, Carol, were living in Dubai in the United Arab Emirates; later he immigrated to Johannesburg, South Africa. In 1972, he happened to be staying with his new wife's family in Gloucestershire and was coming to see mother on my last night in England. I waited with her for a long time but finally gave up and went back to the Running Horses, where I was once again staying, keeping my eye on the door hoping he would come in. Strangely, when he arrived I did not recognize him. But I knew Carol from the pictures Ma had just shown me.

They arrived about 10 p.m. just as the pub was closing. So we got a bottle of champagne and went back to Mother's flat to enjoy it with her. She was happy to have us visit but soon became sleepy and relaxed from the champagne, so Carol, Tony and I drove to Leicester Square in London's West End for a meal together. It was a crazy trip; I felt I was in a race car, careening through the dark streets into London and back to the pub where I was staying. The next day it was back to the U.S.

It had been 24 years since I had seen Tony.

We had hardly communicated at all since I left for America; most of the time I had not known where he was living while he was married to Doreen. Fondly, it was a start of many pleasant visits in many places: England, Oregon, Louisiana (New Orleans), Georgia (Atlanta) in the U.S.A., along with South Africa and the most favorite of ours, France; all to see my brother Tony again.

Tony, Joy and Geoffrey on the Isle of Wight ~ 1985

In October 1980, Carl and I flew to London. My mother was gone and we had told my other English relatives that we were coming. As we planned to have the first three days to ourselves in London, we decided to leave earlier than we had told them. Imagine our surprise when we were waiting for a bus in front of Charing Cross railway station and my Aunt Alice gets off the bus! On our first night!! After nervous explanations of why we were there earlier than we had said, we went back to our hotel. She cancelled her evening art class and we had a lovely visit over glasses of wine, and then walked to the Underground station with her to see her on her way. We enjoyed the time we had in London, but we weren't able to see Geoffrey; he was having a house built on the island and was having problems he couldn't leave untended.

We took the train to Southampton where we embarked for New York on the QE2, a large Cunard luxury ocean liner. Once again, I was on the Atlantic Ocean in grey, cold weather; not quite as stormy as in 1948 but much more comfortable surroundings. The food was wonderful and the surroundings elegant; we had a comfortable trip with lots to eat, movies and other entertainments to watch. We watched the gambling tables but that was way beyond our expertise and budget. It was a restful and relaxing trip, so different to 1948, though the ocean was still overwhelmingly big and not much calmer; the ship was steadier.

Our problems started when we docked in New York. I have never liked that city; even when only changing planes, somehow things always seem to go awry. We went through customs with our bags. We had bought some antiques in England but had no difficulties when declaring them. Outside the customs office the rain was pouring heavens hardest; the roads were flooded and everyone wanted a cab. The police, directing the queue for taxis, questioned our destination and insisted that people going to the same place share cabs. We shared with another couple who were going to La Guardia Airport. The heavy downpour continued; the water so deep it was halfway up the wheels of the cars. Traffic was backed up and bumper to bumper because the freeway we were traveling was flooded; the East River was overflowing its banks.

It took over two hours to get to the airport, usually a 20-minute trip. The taxi driver unloaded the bags and took off. As he drove away, I realized we were short a bag!! It contained several special things: an expensive antique clock, artistic-enameled bracelets and brooches my grandfather had made. Most important of all, it included the engraved invitation and menu from my French grandparent's wedding celebration, held in Angouleme, France on June 27, 1892. I was heartbroken. I tried for months to see if it could be located; no one could help or compensate the loss. I remembered the taxi driver's license number yet the authorities said there was no such license number. I learned later there were many men driving taxis in New York under phony licenses.

It was a thankless task to try to recover the bag, every venture a dead end. To top it off, the storm was so bad no planes were flying that afternoon. After several hours they transferred us by bus to a different airport. A horrible way to end a pleasant trip; it hurts even now. Those wedding papers, given to me by Aunt Alice were so precious to me, such a treasure for my genealogy study of our family. I never told her they were lost or stolen.

During later years, Carl and I took our granddaughters to England; Stephanie when she was ten in 1979, and Stacey when she was 12 in 1986. By then my mother was gone, but I still visited my Aunt and, of course, there is enough in London and the Isle of Wight to keep children occupied: Madame Tussauds Wax Works, the Tower of London, even the wildlife in St. James Park are fun to watch. On the island there were farms and castles that Geoffrey took us to see.

In 1988, I took Stacey to Paris when she was 14, she loved this city and we walked everywhere, enjoying all we saw. We rode on the 'Bateaux Mouches' on the River Seine and went to Versailles on the train. Eating in French restaurants was fun, especially the night we sat by the 'guillotine' they used to cut the baguettes. The waiters would talk to her each time they came by, although she couldn't understand a word. The French are very economical with their electricity and lights in the hallways are on timers. Sometimes you have to be quick to get from your room to the bathroom down the hall before the light shuts off; she had fun! Thank goodness I have enough understanding of the French language to get along okay, and it is helpful but nowadays many Parisians speak English.

What a pleasure it was to travel with young children and to see things through their eyes. They seem to notice so many different details and have interesting (though often unanswerable) questions about everything; it stimulates your own mind to keep up with them. We originally flew into London and visited with my brother, Tony, in his new home in Ledbury, Herefordshire. We spent time in Oxford and then took the train from Victoria Station (London) to Paris arriving at the Gare du Nord (train station). Our hotel was close by and from there we had fun exploring the city, especially the Eiffel Tower. This adventure also included the Louvre, where we saw the famous Winged Victory (a marble sculpture dating before Christ) with beautifully carved wings; unfortunately, the sculpture had lost her arms and head centuries ago. The Louvre is also the home of the Mona Lisa. The white Sacre Coeur Basilica, standing at highest point in Paris, excited Stacey who was fascinated by the crowds on the steps with musicians playing and many novelty salesmen offering trinkets to the tourists, boats on the River Seine, and the long walkways beside the water.

I love going to France and my brother, Tony, was quite fond of it as well. Was this because we had heard so much about it in our young years from our parents and Grandmother Therin? Whenever we visited, Grandma would tell us of her childhood in Angouleme, washing clothes in the river and working in the fields. Except to travel to England to live, I don't think she ever left the small town of her birth. Why my grandfather was in Angouleme I will never know; it has always seemed strange to me that a man from Paris ended up in a place like Angouleme after completing his two compulsory years in the army. One of the high points of my mother's life was when, as a teenager, her father took her to visit his mother in Paris; I don't remember any details she gave. I believe his mother came to England for a visit before World War I. Not much was ever said about her. I do know her name was Louise Therin and later she married Charles Victor Rayel.

In 2007, I went to Paris for several days with my brother, Geoffrey, to discover Paris on foot. Each day we walked in a different direction. One day we passed the building our Great-grandmother Therin had once lived in with M. Rayel. I wondered: Did my mother stay there in her youth when she went with her father to see her?

Daddy would talk about being in the trenches during the war, and he would sing French songs and use French phrases. I had taken five years of French in school and have taken extra classes throughout the years. I have not mastered it as I would like and often freeze up when I first arrive in France; it typically takes me two days to 'thaw out.' I think they speak rapidly, though everyone speaks their own language rapidly. I have to listen very closely to separate the words. However, I manage to enjoy conversations with friends I have made there.

While my mother was still alive, I was focused on her and did not travel anywhere overseas except to England. It took me years to realize how lonely her life had become. Her daughter was in America, her oldest son in South Africa, and even her youngest son was living on an island. The sea separated her from all her children. After returning to her home from her visit with me in America in the fall of 1963, she had moved several times to ensure care as she had difficulty walking. Even after I first went to see her in Erith, she was moved to different grades of care homes according to her needs. The last time I visited her was shortly before her death in 1978.

Since then I have traveled to several countries thanks to having an international family. I visited with my brother Tony, who was living in South Africa, and had bought a summer home in France. My daughter, Vivian, spent many years working in Saudi Arabia and during the Desert Storm War lived with her Air Force husband in Germany. I visited them in Germany and we traveled through several European countries by car: Belgium, Holland, Luxemburg, France, Austria, Lichtenstein and Switzerland. We also made a trip to Italy together on one of our returns from Saudi Arabia. My son, being stationed for years in Hawaii with the U.S. Navy, provided another interesting trip. When my British nephews moored their yacht in Malta on a sailing adventure, I was eager to join them. My lovely sister–in–law, Carol, took me to Spain. My travel agent, Teri, asked me to go to Mexico to assess timeshare condos.

They all gave me lots of opportunities to travel and to stay with friends and family. Geoffrey has taken me to France, and we have stayed in Tony and Carol's residence in the South of France. We would take the ferry across the English Channel and drive south on different routes to their home and stay a couple of weeks. Geoffrey always planned a good route so we could see interesting places including historic buildings and sites as well as beautiful French countryside. Then there was our walking trip in Paris; it was October and the weather was great. Each day we enjoyed the beauty of Paris along with its good food and wine; wish I could do that again!

Geoffrey, Joy, and Tony in France ~ 1993

I was sorry to miss one opportunity. My daughter, Barbara, lived in Turkey for a couple of years when her husband Frank was stationed with the Air Force. It would have been interesting to see the mosques and the grand bazaars and markets. Also Vivian invited me to go to Russia with her, but I had broken my ankle and was unable to travel; it was a disappointment as I am interested in Russian history. Otherwise I have taken every opportunity I have been given to travel overseas. I don't know if I am a tourist or a visitor? I always have somewhere to stay and someone who knows where to go to see the best. I'm so thankful that my family helped me visit so much of the world. It's been a wonderful experience and I certainly never dreamed it would all come from that first long journey to America.

In 1987, after many years running two restaurants and a catering business, I retired from the food industry business. I continued to cater private parties for special friends. Starting in 1982, I catered for opening night parties and special events for the local Salem playhouse, Pentacle Theatre. Except for a couple of long breaks, I carried on with that job until 2008, for 26 years. I have no ability to act but loved working with a wonderful group of devoted volunteers who put on excellent productions for local audiences

In the mid 1990s, I also volunteered for Oregon State Government at both the Capitol Building and Governor's Mansion. In the Capitol, I served as a doorkeeper in the Senate and a greeter at front entrance (when there were sections of the Capitol closed due to earthquake damage). My work as a mansion tour guide when Governor Barbara Roberts resided, allowed me the opportunity to create two historic photo albums for the mansion; one in my home and one that may still be on display in the mansion today. And then I broke my ankle at Smith Rock in 1995, which ended my ability to do this job.

At that time Carl was not in the best of health, and we would sit in our sunroom, admiring our lovely garden, talking and dozing and discussing who was going to fix a sandwich when we got hungry. Having been a heavy smoker since his time in the army, he had breathing problems and was on oxygen.

*Our 50th Wedding Anniversary at our Sunset home of
(then) 38 years ~ April 28, 1995*

Earlier in April, we celebrated our 50th wedding anniversary with a wonderful party at home including family members and friends from both sides of the Atlantic. Carl had been well that day and enjoyed being with the crowd; he never used oxygen or needed a nap. What wonders friends and family can do!

My ankle healed and my brother Geoffrey wanted to meet me in London and go to the South of France to see our brother, Tony, who was also very ill with respiratory problems. With Carl's agreement I left, though reluctantly as I knew he was not doing well. When in London I received the news on October 14, 1995 that he had died. We cancelled the rest of the trip and Geoffrey and I returned to my home immediately; it was sad. All my children were there: two daughters Jennifer and Barbara, living in town; Philip flying in from California; and Vivian from Saudi Arabia to spend time with me as a family. His memorial service and reception at the Eagles club, where he had enjoyed spending time and visiting with his friends for the past few years, was followed by a family gathering at my home.

And what made things more heartbreaking, Tony died three months later to the day, and although I made it to France, he never knew I was there. His and Carol's three children, Anja, Mark and Edward, were there. Maggie, from his first marriage, came and her brothers Michael and Simon were in contact. Tony was cremated in France but a memorial service was held in the small village of Castle Frome, Herefordshire, where they have their English home.

Since my retirement I have worked on tracing my family history and have spent time in London, Angouleme and Paris researching my ancestors. After over 50 years of living in America I had lost trace of all my Beaver and Therin cousins that I knew in the war years, but I have now found them again and have been to England for several reunions.

Top: Barbara, Richard Langstaff, Betty Langstaff Heel,
Alan Beaver, Geoffrey, Reginala Heel, Vivian.
Below: Felicity Langstaff, Carol Beaver, Joy, Doreen (Alan's
partner) ~ 2002

It has been many years, but my tie to England has never broken.

Chapter Thirteen

NEW LIFE IN SALEM

In 2007, I wrote this article comparing the new life I found in America to my years in England. It was published in the Salem Statesman Journal's "Moments of the Past," October-November.

I was a GI war bride, born in England and married to an American soldier in 1945. My husband had lived in Salem, Oregon before joining the army, he liked the town and thought we could enjoy a good life here, so after an extremely rough, fifteen day passage across the Atlantic Ocean, we docked in New York Harbor the day after Valentine's Day 1948. From there we came across the United States by train, through Chicago, on The Portland Rose train to Portland and on to Salem on 99E, riding a Greyhound bus. In those days, Highway 99E was the most direct route between the two towns, passing through very small places like Canby, Hubbard and Woodburn. It was a slow journey, there was no freeway until the 1950s, and then it was only from Aurora north.

The rain bothered me a lot when I came here; though England is noted for its rain and cold winds, here it seems to be heavier. I came here at the time of the Vanport floods in Portland, when whole areas were washed away. Keizer, too, was flooded at that time; all this was before Detroit Dam was built. It also seemed to snow more the first few winters I was here than it does now.

To a young person, who had spent all her life on the outskirts of London, Salem was a shock. In those days, Salem was a very small place. The City of Salem! In England a City always had a cathedral, with a bishop in charge, here there were only a few churches, and most of them were built of wood, some very small places of worship, or meeting halls, with none of the grandeur of European churches. In the late fifties and early sixties many congregations built larger churches. People were very religious here, coming to our door or speaking to us in the store or on the bus, inviting us to join their church.

People were very kind; I was invited to church groups and was introduced to other war brides. I made friends with a girl from Chester, England who lived in Keizer; she had a car and took me to meet other newcomers. We would have tea together and within a few months had formed a war brides club, girls from many different nations and we still get together until this day. The support of those girls, in the same situation as I was, learning new ways, having young children, being homesick and far from family, was the best thing that could have happened. Although I was from England and spoke English all my life, I still had problems with the language. Often pronunciation was different, meanings of words and phrases were entirely opposite at times, a chemist shop is a pharmacy here, a reel of cotton is a spool of thread, there were so many. I got teased a lot when I started working in a restaurant.

I felt Salem was more like a village than a town; there was so much open space around it. From Salem to Keizer, one went past open fields, no Fred Meyers store or NW Natural Gas Company; there were no big churches on Broadway all that came later. Cherry Avenue was very open, often with floodwaters to the west, causing many frogs in the area, and heavy fog on winter nights. On the eastside there was an aluminum plant that was torn down in the fifties.

We lived in a motel in the Hollywood district for a while, as housing was very difficult to find: so many men were coming out of the services, getting newly married and looking for houses and jobs. Many returning soldiers built their own homes in that era, and codes were not as strict. Hollywood district was at the junction of North Capital Street and Fairgrounds Road, the Hollywood theater was there, across from the motel, also several small shops including Slim Hale's jewelry shop, Bob and June Graves 'Lullaby baby shop' selling baby clothes, and a couple of small cafes. I cannot remember a grocery store; I know we would walk north, past the Mayflower Dairy Plant, through the underpass, near the Valley Packing Meat Co. to Carleton Avenue to a super market there.

We walked a lot in those early days in Salem. We didn't have a car, but it was no problem; I had only ridden in a car about six times in my life (my father had always been too ill to drive), and we had lived through six years of war, so we never had owned one, in fact I knew very few people who did. I was accustomed to London's tremendous public transportation system, and thought all towns relied on buses and local trains. There were some buses here, and when we moved to Keizer, we sometimes rode the bus to downtown Salem, but often we walked. One evening walking into Salem, we watched a crane hoist a very large bread oven into an opening made in the brick wall on the top floor of the Master Bread Company on the southwest corner of Broadway and Market. The hole was closed with different color bricks and the site of the opening was obvious until the day the building was torn down in 2005. For many years it housed the Salem Eagles Lodge, now it is gone. Piggly Wiggly grocery was across the street.

Keizer was just a few shops around Keizer Corners, with the Keizer grade school on the northwest corner. At the junction of Cherry Avenue and North River Road there was Coomler and Franz, a hardware store, and Sam Orcutt's grocery store was nearby. North River Road was lined with big old houses, which have nearly all disappeared.

Downtown Salem was an area of a few blocks, Commercial Street to High Street; State Street to Chemeketa Street covered the main shopping area. Before my time, Salem High School was where Macy's (Meier and Frank) now stands. It was a temporary Marion County Court House for a few years and it was there that I received my American citizenship. Salem had several cinemas in 1948, The Elsinore on High Street, The Capitol on State Street, The State on Church Street and one on Commercial Street. The Meadows, the Spa and the Cupboard I on State Street were popular restaurants and Pike's on Liberty Street and Al's on High Street were ice cream parlors. There was a drug store with a soda fountain counter on the corner of High and Court. The Senator Hotel was on High Street, and on the opposite side of the street was the grand old City Hall, with many wide steps leading to the main door, the police department below, and the fire department to the west on Chemeketa Street.

But there were no pubs! England is full of pubs, places where people got together to relax and visit, they often had gardens to sit in and places for children to play. In Salem it was only cafes, restaurants or taverns. In nice restaurants, if customers wanted an alcoholic drink they had to take their own bottle, the bartender poured and charged for service and mix. Liquor by the drink did not come into Salem until 1954.

There were a lot of goods for sale everywhere, after six years of war I had forgotten shops existed where you could find all you wanted. I had a problem with the money; I was not used to the decimal system, and I kept thinking a dollar was the same as an English pound, instead of only one fifth, five dollars to the pound in 1948! Clothes weren't the same either; the New Look had come in. I was amazed in New York to see all the women in ankle length dresses, short jackets and ballerina shoes, in the snow! Back home, very few people rode in cars so we needed heavier clothes because of the weather, trousers were not popular for women, only for war workers; we wore heavy stockings and hand knitted cardigans, mostly old clothes. I wore the same school uniform for five years; we didn't get enough ration coupons to buy new. A baby wore terry cloth napkins (diapers) and long dresses until they were about six months old, boys and girls, their little legs were kept covered, and they were put in prams when taken out.

England was still rationed when I left in 1948 (they were rationed for many things until 1954): food, clothes, furniture, household goods and linens. Then I came to Salem, where grocery shops were jammed with goods and nobody had to line up for hours hoping that they wouldn't sell out before you reached the head of the line, as we had done back in our country. I had to learn to cook when I got here; the choice was overwhelming and tastes were different. Casseroles were acceptable, meals were made with cream soups, Jell-O salads with vegetables folded in, but Christmas puddings and heavy fruitcakes were not popular. There were many differences.

The Oregon coast was beautiful, so "untouched." The road had a few shops and motels, fewer restaurants and fewer high, view-blocking motels than now. It was quaint and not commercialized, but in those days it took a long time to get there, sometimes well over two hours, with older, slower moving cars and winding, narrower roads.

Yes, to those of us who married Americans and came to live here, Salem was very different from our own countries, but mostly in the small things: riding in cars, houses built of wood, many electric kitchen appliances, greater fashion turnover, longer store hours. Now it is all a pleasant memory, and our war brides group often talks of those days, and we are thankful for all the years we've been here in Salem and the U.S.A.

War Bride Tea, March 1949

Salem Accent Club ~ 1949. Joy is 1st row, 2nd from left.

Salem Accent Club ~ 2012. (63 year Coordinator/Hostess Joy is standing)

Chapter Fourteen

MORE MEMORIES OF SALEM LIFE

*I*n 2007, I wrote this article comparing the new life I found in America *to my years in England. It was submitted to the Salem Statesman Journal but unpublished as the column was canceled.*

Once we got a car, we would drive around town, and I was interested in all the new places to explore. Salem became more than the small place I had thought it to be. We had a 1936 Plymouth Coupe; just the front seat with an open space behind, where our children loved to ride along standing up. This was long before anyone thought of seatbelts! We drove the very winding road to Mill City to visit Iris, an English war bride from my hometown. Her husband was working on Detroit Dam; I couldn't believe they buried a town to build it.

There were two hospitals in Salem when I came here in 1948. The Salem General Hospital was on Center Street, just east of 25th street, across from the State Hospital, which was more commonly known as the Insane Asylum. I learned that Center Street was called Asylum Avenue in the 19th century! Salem Memorial Hospital, or the Deaconess Hospital, was located where Salem Hospital is now on Winter Street. I was a patient there once in those early years, and I thought it was like a little cottage; there were four beds in the room and a fireplace!

Traveling west on Center Street, Elmer Berg had a grocery store at the corner of 17th and Center. Shortly after I arrived here, the Capitol

Shopping Center was built at Capitol and Center, and Elmer moved into a much larger store there. Years later, he moved to North River Road in Keizer. Sears Roebuck was on Capital Street, and the Owl Drug Store, among other stores, and it's now a parking lot for State workers. A block north at Capitol and Union was an ice skating rink. East was Washington School at 12th and Center, but it was razed soon after I came to Salem; a Safeway is there now, and the street plan was reorganized. In 1948, there were no one-way streets and not many traffic lights! Across from Parrish Junior High (corner of Capitol and 'D' Streets) there was a little shop; if you drove by just as school was over, you would see lots of children leaving the school and heading there for ice cream at the soda fountain.

All children had worn uniforms to school in England; here they did not, but in their way of dressing they all looked much alike with their poodle skirts, bobby socks and saddle shoes. The school system here was so different to that in England. Here all children went to the same school, kindergarten through age 18. In England we were tested at 11 and were sent to different schools, according to our abilities. Highest scorers, possible college students, went to high school until 16; next were those with mechanical trends sent to technical schools; the rest attended school until they were 14.

12th Street was only a narrow street then; the railway ran alongside with the train depot there. Copeland Lumber was on the west side, and also Walt's Tavern, a popular place! Its entrance was right on the small side-walk; I don't know where customers parked. There were a couple of cafes close by, one on the southeast corner of Leslie Street, and one further south, which may still be in business. In 1948, Mattie Reed and her husband built Reed's Drive-In at 12th and Leslie Street; it later became 'The Broaster,' serving broasted chicken, advertised as 'FingerLickin' Good!' Changes in road planning caused the building, houses and Leslie Street to disappear in that block. Further south was Myers Glove Company; Hazel Myers was a war bride in our group. Her brother and his wife (Fred and Olive) came over from England, and they both worked at the glove company for many years.

I was scared when I saw trains running along main streets: 12th Street, Union Street and Broadway all had tracks. I was surprised that there were no level crossings or train tracks in viaducts or valleys as I had known growing up, just train whistles to warn the people. I was amused years later when the engineer would park his train just north of Broadway and Hood and go into the Wooden Shoe for his morning coffee! I found the crossing at Union on Liberty Street, in a busy part of town, especially dangerous. Even today, I find driving alongside a train nerve-wracking; maybe it's the noise. For years after I came here, the noise of airplanes could upset me.

At the corner of 25th and Mission Street was Water's Park, a baseball field. We went there often in my first few years in this country, and baseball is the only sport I know anything about, thanks to those many evenings watching the Salem Senators play. Sadly, the park burned down, and it was years before Salem had another ball field. My husband would go bowling in an upstairs bowling alley on Ferry Street; he had set pins there during his high school days and was eager to show me something of his life before me! There was also a dance hall on Ferry and Liberty, Crystal Gardens; we never went there but we did take ballroom dancing lessons at a nearby studio. Salem had some popular parades during those after-the-war years and I remember 'The Salem Cherrians' always were featured in them. The men wore white suits and boating hats and red cherries were their emblems.

The Marion Hotel was on Commercial and Ferry, and Gideon Stoltz Brewery was one block south of that; the brewery disappeared with the advent of the new Salem City Hall and its grounds. Weider's Laundry was further east.

Miller's Department Store was fun. It was located on the corner of Liberty and Court, a large store with the very slowest elevator ever; and it had a pneumatic money system! You made your purchase and the clerk enclosed your money and bill in a tube, and inserted it into a system of pipes hanging from the ceiling. The tube whooshed through the pipes quite noisily to the cashier's office up in the mezzanine. She registered the sale and returned your change and receipt by the same route. It was quite fascinating to watch. Across the street was Woolworths, fronted on Liberty and State, with a pharmacy on the corner, making Woolworths a right-angled store, wrapped around Capitol Drug Store, called a chemist shop in England! It had a snack bar on the Liberty street side. Fred Meyers was north of Woolworths, a long narrow shop with very narrow aisles that dead-ended in the south wall. Shopping there was very crowded. Salem had a butcher's shop in those days. Midget Meat Market was in the 300 block of State Street, by the alley. Sides of beef hung in the shop and often the butcher cut your meat to order; it was good to see after years of rationed meat and empty butchers' shops.

Further north on Liberty, between Center and Marion was a Christian Science Church with a large Dome, an impressive building, replaced now by the Salem Mall. Greyhound buses left from the same area as they do now; there were Trailways buses that left from the Senator Hotel, and the city buses left from Commercial and State, in front of Allen's Hardware store, or was it Salem Hardware? My memory fails me. Doughton's Hardware was on Court Street.

Hardware stores were fascinating; they sold my favorite Franciscan 'Desert Rose' dishes which I bought in the early 1950s and still use today. Also, they sold everything imaginable for home repair, boxes and barrels of screws, pipes, washers etc., and wonderful kitchen things, appliances to help with cooking. I hadn't even seen a toaster before I came here; we used a toasting fork over a coal fire. Coal was rationed: No coal, No toast!

I became acquainted with credit buying for furniture. Our first purchase was a refrigerator; it had a meter on it and you put a quarter in it every day to keep it running, and the meter was emptied monthly for the payment. I was really excited; I had never seen a refrigerator in a home before, only in cafes and ice cream parlors in England, or in American movies. I also bought a coat at Kay's Ladies shop on lay-away. I was becoming an American! The Little French shop on High was a wonderful place for ladies fashions, but too exclusive for my budget.

Valley Ford was on the corner of Center and Liberty and every Christmas they had an extremely tall Christmas tree on display in their corner window, completely covered with thousands of silver tinsel threads, a beautiful sight! There was Loder Oldsmobile, Otto J. Wilson Buick, Stan Baker Dodge, and McKay Chevrolet, all in Salem.

My husband pointed out the house he had lived in when his family first came to Salem in 1936. It was on Liberty, two houses south of Karr's tavern, now called Boones Treasury. The house, one of the original houses in Salem, was moved to Mission Mill and is now part of their display of early houses of Salem. Portland General Electric and Seven-up Bottling Company were across a little bridge over Mill Creek, just south of Karr's Tavern and Larmer Transfer, a moving company that was further north.

About 1952, the State of Oregon gave all Oregon servicemen a bonus and we were able to put a down payment on a house, and so I stayed!

And I remember when Market Street was Garden Road beyond Lancaster Drive!

Yes! I remember Salem as it was, so different to England, but a great adventure.

Joy & Carl's Wedding Day ~ April 28, 1945

Joy and Carl with son, Philip ~ 1946

Joy to Carl ~ Happy Birthday ~ June 10, 1945

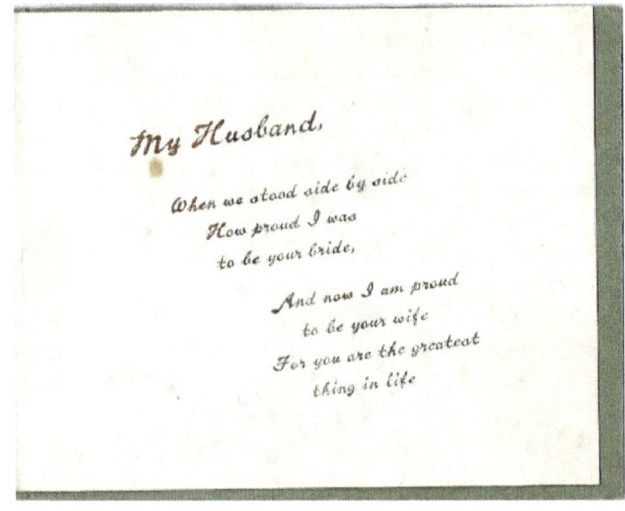

*Carl and Joy's 25th Wedding Anniversary ~
1970*

*Joy and Carl celebrate 50 years among
friends at the Sunset Home ~ 1995*

Renee Therin Beaver 1894 ~ 1978

William James Beaver 1896 ~ 1941

Chapter Fifteen

MOMENTS OF MY WARTIME WEDDING

Yesterday, April 28, 2015, was the seventieth anniversary of my wedding day. Seventy years of memories flooded my mind, wonderful ones of my actual wedding day.

Joy at St. John's Church ~ 2015

It snowed as I went into the church on my brother Tony's arm, dressed in the beautiful wedding dress he found for me...I suspected on the black market, but he never ever shared his secret! White satin high-heeled shoes, too, no "Utility" war-time shoes for his sister! The church had been badly bombed in recent air raids; all the windows had been blown out and were now patched up with plywood. The tiles on the roof were shattered and the new snow was melting and dripping through the rafters into buckets on the floor making little pinging sounds.

Halfway down the aisle, I had to stop as my veil caught on the shattered wood floor and was coming loose. Repairs were made and soon the service proceeded, but when the vicar started to say 'with this ring I thee wed'... Carl could not slide the ring onto my finger...the vicar, a down to earth fellow, said 'spit on it Carl' and so I was married.

We were a small family group. I had three young bridesmaids and my mother had used precious clothing coupons to buy pink and blue fabric for the dresses she made for them. They looked so pretty, although a little shy. My father had died a couple of years before and so had my paternal grandparents. My mother was not very friendly with the rest of Daddy's family, so they were not invited but her mother (my grandma) and her two younger sisters came, as well as my brothers and some of our neighbours. As we left the church the sun was shining and the parking area was full of American soldiers in uniform cheering us and taking pictures...along with a few local girls. As per wartime rationing, we were allowed only 3 photos by the photographer, all of which are included in this book. We received some of the other photos from the GIs who took them, but in one photo I was cut off, and in another photo Carl was cut off. As well, the photos were tiny—about 1½ inches square.

We went back to our house on Marlborough Road for a small reception in our rarely used front drawing room. Little tea sandwiches and our wedding cake set on a 'broiderie anglaise' tablecloth of my grandmother's. It was a genuine English wedding cake, which after almost six years of war was unbelievable. English wedding cakes were fruitcake and we had not seen such ingredients for seemingly ever! It was Tony's gift again! What A Special Brother he was!

My younger brother Geoffrey was not quite eleven at this time and his thrills were more personal; brand-new shoes and his first pair of long trousers! Long trousers held a special place in this young English boy's life. After suffering cold knees and scratchy socks for years; he could finally take his place among the grown-ups. His greatest memory of that day was the water dripping steadily from the arched roof of the church into the metal buckets on the floor.

My mother hired a car to take us to the church and now it was to take us to the railway station, where we caught a train to Arundel for a weekend honeymoon. We had a lovely quiet weekend together while ignoring the world. We admired the peaceful countryside, old castles and grand houses, and were thankful there were no signs of rubble or bomb damage. We were together.

But the world was stirring...the world was crazy! The unbelievable had happened! Adolf Hitler, Chancellor of Germany, the probable cause of this long, devastating war had married his long-time girl friend, Eva Braun, killed her and then he killed himself. And people celebrated! Other Nazi German officials also committed suicide and some escaped, and we wondered what was in store for us...would there be retaliation?

Within days the war was over. Prisoners among Nazis leaders were taken, concentration camps were discovered and liberated, and it seemed impossible that such terror and devastation could end so unexpectedly. We were joyful and we cheered, but still found it hard to believe.

Carl had a weeks' leave coming, so we prepared for a visit to a seaside town, ready to leave on May 8th 1945. It was 'Victory in Europe' Day, V.E. Day forever! That day people did not go to work, and their hoarded rations were used to celebrate, to feed friends and families, and beer was plentiful. Quiet or rowdy street parties were organized, depending on your neighbourhood, bonfires were lit and Hitler effigies were burned. Shops were closed, buses did not run, and train schedules were disrupted. THE WAR WAS OVER!!

Carl and I were trying to get a train to Brighton on the south coast and had to wait patiently for hours to find transportation. No riotous celebration in Piccadilly Circus or in the pub, just quiet togetherness on a railway station. The war is over; what now?

Brighton was lovely in May. We were in a comfortable bed and breakfast, and food was much better there than city food had been. They grew their own, farms were nearby where they raised animals and they had fresh seafood from boats on their own shore. The shops were more interesting with hand made goods and lots of flowers, as they had not had nearly as much war time disruption as London had suffered.

Churches were always open for the comfort of the people, and they had never locked their doors during the war.

I was disappointed that the Prince Regent's Palace (the Prince of Wales' seaside resort) was becoming derelict and was no longer open to the public. The Prince Regent became George IV when his father died and he was on the English throne from 1820-1830. He was a good-looking king, sociable but unreliable, yet was regent for ten years before succeeding to the throne. Just seeing the site stirred my love of England's history.

After a week in Brighton, we returned to the chaos of after-the-war London. Within weeks it was decided that the 6811th Signal Corps, Carl's outfit was needed for code– breaking in Germany where they could intercept messages from the Japanese, who were still at war with the Allies.

One sad day, I watched their long convoy form at Hall Place in Bexley, where they were stationed, travel to the motorway and head for the coast of England on their journey through France and into Germany.

Every man and every trace of equipment was gone with only debris left behind. It was the end of an era, of fame for Hall Place, which had been their home for over two years.

Life changed and much happened in the ensuing decades, but fifty years later our togetherness was celebrated with dozens of friends and family shortly before Carl died. It was the end of an era of our lives together.

Chapter Sixteen

70-YEAR WEDDING DRESS JOURNEY
APRIL 28, 1945 ~ 2015

I was able to keep the silk buttoned, white satin wedding dress, though because of hard times, the veil had to be returned. What happened to the beautiful bouquet? I believe it was laid on Daddy's grave in Chislehurst Cemetery nearby, where my Granny Beaver is also buried in the quiet area under the trees. I wish they could have been at the wedding to see me holding such beautiful flowers.

There were marks from the flowers and stains from the Church's wooden floor on the dress, but it was just put away with no real plans.

The 1940s cleaners on Bexleyheath Broadway had been badly bombed during one of the air raids and was out of business, so there was no way to get the marks removed. The dress was just special to me and I treasured it. It was more than a wedding gown; it represented a dramatic change of life, an indelible memory of my oldest brother's attention to me and a journey to a faraway foreign land, America.

10 days before Victory in Europe ~ May 8, 1945

When I finally agreed to travel to and live in the United States, the satin gown was packed in our big tin trunk with our other goods for the long journey. I knew so little about packing that I threw everything in the trunk and in not too good an order; even dishes were wrapped in our clothes. We had no newspaper to wrap them in as it was a terribly scarce commodity during the war years. Even though the war was now over, only the bombardment and gunfire had disappeared. We were left rationing food, clothes, petrol, furniture and most goods. You could get special coupons for sheets and towels when you got married, but even people married a long time were still trying to get by with pre-war belongings. Life was really austere!

By the time our trunk reached Salem, everything in it was broken and buried in china shards destroyed by sea storms, rough handling, and poor packing. What could I expect? I cried hysterically yet amazingly, my wedding dress weathered the storm, ironically untouched.

It hung in my closet for years. Once there was an article in the newspaper about Deepwood Estate on Mission Street in Salem having a display of early era wedding dresses, but mine did not fit their criteria. They were hoping for Salem bridal gowns of pre-war days.

So back to the closet again yet, this time, not before going to the cleaners and packed into an airtight bag ... poor dress! I still could not part with it. My girls did not choose to wear it; in fact, my youngest daughter made her wedding gown spending hours sitting on the couch hand sewing the beaded decorations.

In 2012, I collected written stories about my life and growing up in London during the bombing raids and difficult days of World War II. I published my memoirs as a book, sending it to my children and dear relatives in England so they would receive it on my 67th wedding anniversary. They all seemed pleased to receive "Snapshots of a War Bride's Life" that started an avalanche of attention that has not yet stopped.

My son sent me the Web site address for the National War Brides Association, which we joined. My daughter, Barbara, heard about a national campaign for the WWII Generation called "Keep the Spirit of '45 Alive" and immediately became involved. Within months she became their Oregon Representative and worked to get a bill through the Oregon Legislature to recognize the second Sunday in every August, honoring the "Greatest Generation" at the end of World War II, VJ Day. In August 2012, we joined the Alamo Honor Flight WWII veterans from Texas as they gathered in Baltimore. We shared several days of stories, laughter and tears on their once-in-a-lifetime courtesy visit to Washington D.C. and touring the WWII and other memorials.

Meanwhile, Barbara had contacted the historian of our Capitol City news, Statesman Journal, Capi Lynn. Capi came to interview me about my book. When she heard that I still had my wedding dress, she insisted on seeing it and, for the first time in years, it came out of its airtight bag with this historian counting all the silk-covered buttons! On the Sunday of Memorial Day weekend, the dress covered the front news page with me holding in my hand and heart, wonderful memories.

Statesman Journal, Salem, Oregon ~ 2012

I could not believe such results. I was asked to bring the satin gown to New York City for display in Times Square as we campaigned for the Spirit of '45 at the Jumbotron in front of Walgreen's Drug store. We later were escorted into their large recreation room where a luncheon buffet was held. As well, the dress drew the attention of Good Morning America's Josh Elliott in Times' Square earlier in the day.

Wall Street Journal, NYC ~ 2012

Soon, the dress was on its way to Boston where it was beautifully displayed on a mannequin, alongside four other war bride dresses at our annual War Bride's reunion. It was then back home to the closet again, more regally wrapped in a see-through plastic bag.

Barbara, Vivian, and Joy ~ 1969

Another year went by and once again I was asked to send the dress away in September 2013; this time to the National World War II Museum in New Orleans, Louisiana where all three of my daughters, Jennifer, Barbara and Vivian joined me. What a surprise for me when I arrived at our second National War Brides Reunion. It looked gorgeous, my dress, WOW! Once more, there were three other wedding dresses from the same era; one from Belgium, another from Japan, and the other made from a discarded silk parachute, a fabric often used by those who managed to capture one!

National WWII Museum, New Orleans ~ 2013

In England we were subjected to clothes rationing long after the war was over. We counted our coupons, saving them only for much need work clothes...and shoes! Mothers of American soldiers sent nylons and underclothes from America to their son's English girlfriends; we were thrilled and thankful. One of my fellow war brides recently suggested that I donate my dress to the museum as she had done, but the curator told me it would be kept in storage and used only for special events. I could not part with it. Once again, it travelled back home and into a new upper-grade, see-through bag thanks to my youngest daughter, Vivian.

70th Anniversary of WWII Exhibit ~2014-15. Joy's legacy
remains on permanent exhibit, Hall Place, England.

Early in the fall of 2013, I received an e-mail requesting a copy of my book from a Bob Peterson in Colorado. Upon inquiry, I found out that he had been in the 6811 Signal Corps, the same unit that my husband had served in during the war. Although Bob had joined the 6811th many years after WWII, he was interested in tracing their signal corps history, especially at Hall Place in Bexley, Kent.

This south of London 16th century Tudor home, once an 18-month military site that secretly housed 190 GI code breakers (one of which was my future husband, Carl) from 1943-1945, was organizing an exhibition to honor their long-awaited success story that helped to curtail WWII by two years.

As time passed, I corresponded with Bob, as well as with Priscilla MacPherson of the British National Trust, and Kirsty Macklin, Hall Place museum curator. These history experts encouraged me to join this 70th Anniversary Commemorative Exhibit. For Bob I provided addresses and for Kirsty, I mentioned I still had my wedding dress. She was so pleased and encouraged me to put it into the exhibit. So, once again this 70-year-old, well-preserved and nicely packaged gown returned by air, not sea, back to England to be displayed in the country of its origin. It was encased in a lovely glass display box with my book at its hem.

My dress had brought me back to my hometown and the opportunity to enter, tour and be a part of Hall Place, where no civilian could enter during the war... the place that brought my husband to my corner of the world and into my life.

70th Anniversary of WWII, Hall Place, Bexley, England
~ 2014-15

About the Author

Joy Alicia Beaver Beebe

Joy A. Beebe, a resilient English girl, faced the trials of adolescence amidst the bombing and blitz of London during World War II. Her tenacity and courage were tested as she navigated through the challenging times of 1939-1945. In the midst of chaos, destiny brought her an unexpected love story—a union with an American GI.

After marrying her American sweetheart on April 28, 1945, Joy embarked on a new journey across the Atlantic, settling in the picturesque landscapes of West Coast America, Oregon, in 1948. This marked the beginning of her remarkable life in the United States.

Joy's strength and determination paved the way for her success as a businesswoman. Her entrepreneurial spirit thrived, and she became an integral part of the local community. Over the years, she earned numerous titles, reflecting her dedication to both her professional endeavors and the well-being of those around her.

For an impressive 75 years, Joy called the same town home—a testament to her deep roots and unwavering commitment to her community. Her residence, a witness to decades of memories, stood as a symbol of stability and continuity in her life.

As a loving matriarch, Joy raised four children and found herself surrounded by the warmth of four generations of her family. Her home became a haven of love, laughter, and cherished moments that spanned across decades.

Not content with merely building a thriving family, Joy extended her caring nature to others. She took charge of coordinating activities for local war brides, fostering camaraderie and support among those who shared similar wartime experiences. The Salem Accent Club, another testament to her sense of community spirit, bore the mark of Joy's dedication to fostering connections among its members.

In the latter part of her life, Joy's commitment reached a national level as she served on the board of the National War Brides Association. Her years of tireless effort contributed to preserving the stories and experiences of war brides across the country.

Joy's legacy echoes through the generations of friends and family she left behind in Oregon. Her impact extends across the Atlantic, where her husband's code-breaking legacy and her wedding dress, displayed in a glass case, find a place of honor in the Great Hall of Hall Place and Gardens in England.

Although Joy peacefully passed away in October of 2022 in her home of 65 years, her 97-year enduring legacy lives on—a testament to the strength, resilience, and love that defined her extraordinary life.

Joy's Well-Deserved Titles

(1925 ~ 2022)

Joy Beebe, 1925-2022

- Worldwide Traveler, 74 Years

- Lead Coordinator/Hostess, Salem Accent Club, 70 years

- Lifetime Member/Caterer, Salem Pentacle Theater, 30 years

- Owner, Salem Airport & Keizer Restaurants, 25 years

- Lifelong Learner, Chemeketa CC, French & Writing, 20 years

- Chaperone, Mid-Willamette Valley SnoBall Dance, 10+ Years

- Landlord, On Sunset and Downtown Salem

- Author, Snapshots of a War Bride's Life, published 2012

- Spokeswoman, National Spirit of '45, 10 years

- Spokeswoman, Oregon Spirit of 45, 10 Years

- Teacher's Aide, Salem-Keizer School District, 10 years

- Sunshine Lady, National WWII War Brides, 7 years

- Historian and Guide, Oregon Governor's Mansion, 3 years

- Fashion Model, Salem Lipman's Department Store, 2 years

- Dance Partner w/husband—who didn't dance when they met

- Daughter, Sister, Mom, Sister-In-Law, Ma Beeb, My Mrs. Beebe

- G-ma Joy, G-G-ma Joy, G-G-G-ma Joy, Auntie Joy, Mrs. Joy, Miss Joy

Caretaker to many ... dear friend to all

More about Joy

Joy with her gown

Scan the QR Code with your smartphones camera to view the link

WWII Sir Tony Robinson HOB – War Bride Joy
BBC History of Britain (UK, January 2020)

British Women become GI Brides, Joy Beebe War
Bride Story Kate Thompson

The GIs Who Swept a Nation's Women Off Their
Feet YOU Magazine (UK, December 2021)

Group Captures Spirit of Oregon's WWII Veterans
Military Families Magazine, (US, December 2022)

Rest in Peace Joy, War Bride Tribute Kate Thompson
Tribute (UK, November 2022)

Iconic Kiss Statue Mosaic, Times Square, New York
City, 2012